WILL COLLEGE
PAY OFF?

WILL COLLEGE PAY OFF?

A Guide to the Most
Important Financial Decision
You Will Ever Make

Peter Cappelli

PUBLICAFFAIRS
New York

To Virginia

Library of Congress Control Number: 2015934542
ISBN 978-1-61039-526-7 (PBK)
ISBN 978-1-61039-527-4 (EB)

First Edition

10 9 8 7 6 5 4 3 2 1

Contents

Introduction

College Myths and College Realities

A FOUR-YEAR college education is one of the most important experiences in adult life. What it looks like today, however, is quite different than what most adults remember from their own experience. It is less likely to be a four-year experience on a campus and more likely to be something spread out over many years, often across different colleges, and frequently delivered in office parks. It costs a lot more than it used to, more than in any other country in the world. Far more students are going to college now, especially those from families with fewer advantages, and they often pay for it by taking out loans, sometimes a lot of loans.

In part because of the costs, the pressure has been on colleges to persuade students and their parents that their students will get good jobs when they graduate. To do that, they have responded with a plethora of degree programs that sound just like job titles, such as "international hospitality management," especially at the new and growing for-profit colleges.

At the same time, the message from the media, from the business community, and even from many parts of the government has been that a college degree is more important than ever in order to have a good career. As a result, families feel even more pressure to send their kids to college. This is at a time when more families find those costs to be a serious burden.

For those families, sending their kids to college is a huge investment, and they are making that decision with almost no information as to whether it will pay off or bankrupt them. No one should think that is a good idea. Even the most strident advocates for college education recognize that the experience these days can be wildly different depending on which school and degree program one attends. The graduates of some programs move on to do fabulously well in their careers, although how much of that success is the result of attributes they had even before college is rarely discussed. Graduates of other programs do so poorly afterward that there is no chance they will ever pay off the investment they made to attend these colleges.

We should not kid ourselves about the risks associated with the biggest financial decision many families will ever make. Investments in college fail to pay off because students fail to graduate or when those who do take many years to finish as most now do. They fail when students who graduate with substantial loans cannot earn enough to pay back those loans, many of which come with substantial fees, with interest that compounds the day they are issued, and at interest rates up near the level of car loans. They fail when the good jobs promised by the admissions offices do not materialize. They also may fail even when graduates get a job but when their years on campus were so oriented to job training to get them that first job that they learned nothing that will help them later in the workforce.

Public policy plays a role in these developments. The cutback in funding for public colleges, which most U.S. students attend, pushed the problem of paying for college onto families and continues to do so as the run-up in state college tuition vastly exceeds that of their private school counterparts. The more serious concern going forward may be the effort at state and local governments to make college increasingly vocational, to push students toward degrees that sound like jobs employers are trying to fill.

What is so troubling about this move toward making job training the mission of four-year college programs is that there is no evidence that it works. Employers are certainly interested in what college grads know, but the evidence is striking that what matters most to them are the general abilities and skills that one learns in any serious degree program, including liberal arts. They are least interested in the job-specific knowledge that the new vocational programs are pushing. When students are taking courses in the fine points of healthcare administration, classes that taught more general skills that might be useful over a lifetime, such as logic and problem-solving, are pushed aside.

What prompted me to write this book was the unqualified statements about the big payoff to a college degree that are pushing so many students and their families who can't afford to do so to jump into the deep end of college expenses, taking on debt that they cannot afford for experiences that are unlikely to pay off. While there are lots of guides to tell us whether a particular school suits the temperament of our child, there is almost nothing that helps us decide whether a college experience will lead to financial ruin. That is what I try to offer here, a guide to the factors that determine whether a particular program will pay off.

Along the way, I hope to dispel some of the myths associated with college and the labor market, such as the idea that there is some short-fall of science, technology, engineering, and math or STEM graduates, that college students just won't major in the fields where jobs are, or that jobs today require more education than in the past. I highlight the bigger issues that underlie the payoff from a college degree, such as how much of the success of college grads comes from the ability to identify students who are already very able, how the job market has changed in ways that make work experience rather than education the key factor, and what is happening with K–12 education in the United States that has changed the college marketplace.

Many people helped with this project. Larry Liu provided extremely thorough assistance identifying sources, my colleagues Bob Zemsky, Pat Rose, and Peter Eckel read early drafts and offered suggestions as did Stephen Sherret. Special thanks to John Wright for putting the project together and to my editor John Mahaney for helpful guidance along the way.

1

Why Do People with More Education Get Better Jobs?

The Link Between Education and a Good Job

REPORTS IN THE business press about a shortage of engineers and scientists and charges from the president of the United States for every student to commit to at least some college education make it seem downright patriotic to send your kids to college. The problem is, none of those people saying that more kids should go to college are offering to pay for it. For many families, sending their kids to college is a huge expense that taxes their ability to meet other important needs, such as their retirement. Is it going to be worth it?

There are many great things about going to college. We make friends, often find life partners, learn about life and the world beyond us, and oh yes, take away a bunch of things from classes as well. One aspect of college has become increasingly important, though, and that is getting a job afterward. The reason for that is in part because the costs of college have risen precisely at a time when the weak economy has left so many families unable to pay for it and also because prospects for students who don't go to college have collapsed, at least compared to the previous generation.

While the United States does not lead the world in the proportion of students who graduate from college—the Soviet Union long held that title, and now it is Korea—in no other country do individuals pay so much for college and go in so many numbers. Students in the

5

United States pay about four times more than their peers in countries elsewhere, and more than 70 percent of our high school grads go on to college.

The idea that college is the path to a better life is firmly rooted in the American psyche. Government policies like the GI Bill, the rise of state universities, and federally backed financial aid were all designed to create more opportunity for people with less money to advance in society. The idea that college educations pay off in the form of much higher wages has also been the justification for having individuals and their families pay for it: You should pay because you are going to benefit from it.

In this new environment, college is still accepted as necessary for advancement but also increasingly expensive and increasingly risky in terms of the likely career payoffs. We can attribute a lot of the struggle that new graduates face in getting their careers going to the lingering effects of a weak job market since the Great Recession, but other factors might be at work as well. The sociologists Joseph Arum and Josipa Rocksa interviewed a thousand or so recent graduates and found large numbers of them struggling to get reasonable jobs and more generally to move into adult roles. Arum and Rocksa suspect that something about the preparation the graduates got in college— and perhaps didn't get—may be a poor match for the challenges of modern life.[1]

Something profound does seem to be afoot in that transition between college and adult life, and it has to do with jobs. The time when employers would scoop up new graduates and give them the skills that would make them into lifelong employees is over. Instead, employers are now looking for new hires who already have the skills to start contributing, and they are very picky about who they hire. In the process, they are pushing the problem of getting job skills onto the students, and the students are not doing very well at it.

Almost two-thirds of recent graduates report that they don't have a job that is closely related to their field of study. More than one in five report that they received no information about the job market in college. Almost one in four already believe that their education was not worth the financial costs.[2]

There has been a huge and puzzling campaign arguing that employers have difficulty getting the skills they need and that the problem is with the education system, including college. Some part of that has been driven by lobbying on immigration, mainly by employers in the information technology industry who want the government to allow them to bring in more immigrant workers from lower-wage countries. Some of the media interest in the idea that skills are in short supply has been driven simply by the "man bites dog" situation that with so many people out of work, the fact that employers would claim to have a hard time finding good applicants to hire is newsworthy. All the stories seem to put the solution to the problem on students: Just get the right degree, and you're off and running.

That common view is simply wrong. Students are knocking themselves out trying to figure out where the jobs will be, something that no one can predict with any certainty, and employers actually seem relatively uninterested in academic skills. They want the skills that come from experience on the job, the kind that they used to provide with their own internal training programs.

With all this attention directed at the employer's perspective, virtually no one is thinking about what all this means for students thinking about college and their families who have to pay for it. And that will be my focus here.

Students and their parents know something has changed about hiring, and they look desperately to colleges to help them solve the problem. The colleges have been happy to oblige, or at least happy to assure the families that they can get these young students the skills that will lead to good careers when they graduate. The problem is that we do not know whether their assurances are credible.

The evidence is overwhelming that college graduates have earned more money than high school graduates, but that overall, average evidence obscures important facts. There is a huge amount of variation in outcomes across colleges: Students in some programs do spectacularly well after they graduate, but many others would have been better off financially by not going at all. What do we make of that?

The answer is that one size does not fit all, and a lot of judgment calls are required to get a good outcome from college. Think about the analogy with medicine. For every prescription drug, there is clear evidence that it has the desired effects on average, but we still require that every dose be administered by a licensed expert—your doctor— who has to decide whether the benefits of it in your situation are worth the potential side effects and increasingly whether those bene- fits are worth the financial costs of the treatment. When it comes to college, though, we have none of that expert guidance. We are asked to go with average results for the population as a whole.

We don't have a good sense of exactly why students who attend college on average do better in the job market after. Is it really because of what they learned and experienced in college, or is it because kids who can get into college already have advantages that those who don't go won't have and that graduation demonstrates abilities that are valuable and would have been useful in the job market even if they had not gone to college? If that seems unreasonable, ask yourself how much you grew up between age eighteen and twenty-two: We often attribute that development to college, but a lot of it may have hap- pened anyway. When we compare college grads to new high school grads, we often forget that the former are older, and four additional years at age eighteen make a heck of a difference.

What we do know is that the odds of a good payoff are better in some places than others, and while we cannot guarantee that the bets on a successful career after college will pay off, we can improve the odds with the right decisions.

The focus in this book is to remind us that college is for many people the biggest financial decision they will ever make. It costs a lot, just graduating is far more difficult than most people think, and there are no guarantees about getting a job after. So the risks are big. Many families struggle mightily to pay for the education of their children, often putting other obligations, such as the retirement of the parents, at risk to do so. Paying for college may well mean not paying for something else that also has great value to the family. The relevant question should not just be whether there are benefits with graduating from college—surely there are—but also whether the financial benefits of those degrees are actually worth the cost of attending college.

The recent grad Kyle Laffin, for example, needed his father to co-sign a loan to pay for an undergraduate degree in accounting, a pretty marketable field. And he did get a job, one paying $40,000 per year. But he's got $14,400 in loan payments as well, and his dad is dipping into his retirement to help pay for them.[3] We often don't think about the costs of these loans, but as we will see later, many of them have interest rates that are quite high, the interest accumulates even in college and if you can't find a job after, and even bankruptcy can't get you out from under them. Whether college pays off on average is not that comforting to someone about to roll the dice with the family nest egg on an investment that is hard to assess, that many things can go wrong with, and that even in the best circumstances may not really pay off for a decade or more.

For most families, the question is not so much college versus no college. For all kinds of good reasons, they want their kids to go to college. The question, though, is still which degree, which major, and which college to attend, and for that decision, the possible payoff from the degree matters even more. For other students and their families, college is first and foremost about getting a good job afterward. They cannot afford to attend if that doesn't happen.

Colleges have responded to the concerns about getting a job with a massive shift toward programs that promise to provide job skills that will get students jobs after they graduate. Will employers actually value the increasingly vocational skills in programs like health care administration or construction management? The evidence we will see shortly suggests that they probably don't.

Whether the job that students want will be there four years (or more) after they start is increasingly unclear. Even if graduates get that first job they want, which is typically all we hear about, what happens later? Will the value of a very applied degree designed to give them the job skills to get their first job dissipate, leaving the graduate with something like a career dead end? Would students have been better off with more traditional academic courses, in which at least they learned some general skills, and less vocational classes targeted to a specific field, especially given that there is no guarantee that there will be jobs in that field years later at graduation? Where can we find evidence about the payoff from a particular degree program to help us decide, and if we see it, can we believe it?

What is becoming the prevailing wisdom, that students should be pursuing practical, job-oriented majors like animation, property management, or invasive cardiovascular technology (yes, these are real undergraduate programs), may well be exactly the wrong advice. These narrow, vocational degrees lock students into a single occupation, and they often have to make that decision at age seventeen when they apply to college. They may change their interests and want to switch fields, which may be hard to do in these practical programs. If the jobs aren't there at graduation, their narrow degree might make it difficult to do anything else.

We should also care about more than the first job out of college, as it might not last very long. Many of the high-paying jobs for new grads in fields like engineering and information technology have long-term prospects that aren't very attractive because the skills go out of date quickly and the jobs don't lead to obvious career progression later on. One reason why these jobs don't have such good long-term prospects is because employers can go back to campuses every year and hire new grads with even more up-to-date skills.

The fact that college educations are the biggest expense many families will make is not new, although it is increasingly true for more families. What is new is that it can be the riskiest investment they will make, in part because the job market is less predictable and in part because new ways of paying for it—loans—increase the downside risk if there is no good job at the end. The decisions about college don't have to be guesswork. We can have a much better sense of whether a college degree is going to pay off for any particular student by understanding the important decisions that determine the financial costs and the financial outcomes and what we know from real evidence about them.

The College Context

The United States traditionally sent more kids to colleges than any other country. There are 2,700 four-year colleges in the United States and also almost 4,000 two-year colleges. Under the broad heading of "postsecondary"—after high school—there is now an array of college-like options that did not exist a generation ago, including for-profit colleges, vocational schools that provide all kinds of skill certificates, community colleges and junior colleges with associate degrees, and traditional four-year colleges offering bachelor's degrees in highly specific fields such as health care finance or casino administration. Our focus here will be on college and four-year degree programs, but it is important to note that a huge proportion of students attend other kinds of college.

Higher education's advocates like to point out that if we think of survival as being a sign of success, colleges must be doing something right because most of the oldest institutions in the world are colleges and universities. Several like the Universities of Paris and Bologna and Oxford are closing in on their 1,000th anniversary. A business that fails wouldn't elicit much attention, with the exception of huge corporations like Enron, but it is rare that we see a college close its doors. Many of the ones that do close are the for-profits that only recently started up, like Corinthian Colleges, which shut down a number of its campuses in 2014 under pressure from state and federal regulators.

The business world has undergone rapid transformation over the past several decades. If Tom Rath, the main character of Sloan Wilson's 1955 bestseller *The Man in the Grey Flannel Suit*, wandered into the offices of, say, Google or Apple today, he would be bewildered. But plop a student from Yale a century ago onto that campus today and—with the exception of getting used to a lot of electronic gadgets—he would feel right at home: Dormitories, lectures, clubs, and sports and a great many courses where the titles, and in some cases the content as well, have remained largely unchanged for generations. The lack of change is a source of pride for many colleges.

But things are changing around the traditional model of a four-year residential college, where students learn well-established lessons from the academic world as well as life lessons from their peers. Nowhere are the changes more obvious than in the relationship between the college experience and the job market that students experience when they graduate.

Before the First World War, college was a rare experience reserved for the children of families with considerable means. Being a college graduate was a sign that you were already successful, having been born into the right family. Philanthropists began to start new universities and change that model in the late 1800s—John D. Rockefeller and the University of Chicago and a series of eponymous schools like Cornell, Duke, and Carnegie-Mellon. The Morrill Act in 1862 created the idea of state universities, although college enrollments remained relatively small until after World War II when the GI Bill paid the expenses for returning veterans to go to college, ballooning enrollments. Shortly thereafter, the states expanded their university systems enormously, keeping tuition low enough to make college affordable for virtually any high school graduate who had the ability and motivation to go.

The education-to-career model in those days was simple. We might think of it as a pipeline because the path through it was so predictable: Do well in high school, apply to a four-year college and, if lucky, get into the flagship university in your state system, graduate in four years, and line up to meet the employers who hired graduates into careers that would last a lifetime. At least through the 1960s, the number of jobs available for such graduates typically exceeded the number of graduates, so there was a scramble to hire students, especially the good ones. *Fortune* magazine described the scene in 1948: "Corporate men who work the college circuit for likely executive material— 'ivory hunting' in the trade jargon—complain that the market has never been so unruly. Prices are up at least 100 percent over 1941, and students ... are having a wonderful time playing hard to get."[4] In a hiring frenzy not unlike that associated with the 1990s Internet boom, corporations sent their most impressive executives to recruit students, offering country club memberships and limousine services to lure recruits. This scramble for talent paid off for the companies because those new hires remained with the company for a lifetime, and of course it paid off for the employees as well.

The labor market for graduates softened considerably in the 1970s in part because of the huge influx of baby boom graduates. But the basic model of large employers hiring for potential and training new hires for long-term careers still held. The lifetime-employment model eroded in the early 1980s with the rise of layoffs as the means to restructure companies, but the college-to-career part was still recognizable. Corporations might have been laying off older white-collar workers, but they were still hiring them in from college.

I described what happened next in my book *The New Deal at Work*. Companies that were downsizing, the ubiquitous expression for layoffs, asked themselves why they were maintaining expensive recruiting, training, and development programs for new hires. The glut of experienced white-collar job seekers caused by these layoffs was a boom to any company that was interested in hiring and an alternative to that earlier "grow your own" model. The new darling of the business world was Silicon Valley and its business model of churning through a workforce, hiring experienced talent only when it was needed and then letting that talent go as soon as it was not needed. Companies like IBM, GE, and Hewlett-Packard that still made big investments in employees became the hunting ground for search firms and recruiters looking for talent for companies that did not want to make those investments. Many of those companies started to ask themselves whether that internal model was still worth it. As one CEO told me at the time, "Why should I train my employees when my competitors are willing to do it for me?"[5]

There are two effects associated with this change. The first is the general decline of the entry-level career path where hiring took place from college into jobs where graduates really weren't expected to have any real job skills yet and vacancies in the company were always filled from within. Evidence from large companies a generation or more ago found that 90 percent or so of open jobs were filled from within, through promotions or transfers of existing employees. The other 10 percent were entry-level jobs filled by recent grads, both high school and college. Just before the Great Recession in 2008, however, only about 28 percent of job openings in those large companies were filled from within. When they had openings, they looked outside for candidates who had already done that job or something very similar elsewhere.

With all this outside hiring, it is not surprising that the average time that an employee spends with an employer has fallen. According to the Bureau of Labor Statistics, the number of years a typical employee remains with an employer fell to about 3.5 years in 2000, although it rose considerably after that as the economy slowed, as less-senior workers were laid off and new ones were not hired. As my colleague Matthew Bidwell has shown, the declines in tenure over recent decades have been especially great in the large employers that had provided those long-term careers.[6]

The other development has to do with training. After World War II, it was common for employers to put new college hires into training programs that lasted *years*. Those programs began with classroom education on business and management basics or the equivalent in other fields, progressed to short-term job assignments that rotated across fields to give new hires exposure as well as experience, and included along the way coaching, mentoring, and every other practice that seems cutting-edge today.

The information we have on employer-provided training in the United States now is stunningly poor, probably the worst in the developed world. The data we do have suggest that in 1979 young workers received on average about 2.5 weeks of training per year. By 1991, U.S. Census data found that only 17 percent of all employees reported that they received any formal training that year. Several surveys of employers around 1995 indicated that somewhere between 42 percent of employers offered training that could be described as systematic, and 90 percent reported doing at least some training for someone, with the amount of training an individual received per year averaging just under eleven hours. The most common training topic was workplace safety.[7] The figures also include whatever training vendors provide when they bring in new equipment: "Here's how to work this copier."

These data are now almost twenty years old, and government sources have provided little new data. In 2011, the consulting firm Accenture surveyed U.S. employees and found that only 21 percent had received *any* employer-provided formal training in the previous five years. To be clear, that means almost 80 percent had received no training in five years, and no doubt many of those had received no training in the years before that either. We think of Europe as being a place where there is great training, a lot of it mandatory, but about one-third of employers on that continent also reported that they did not provide training. The main reason they gave for not training was that they tried to hire workers with skills so that they did not need to train. Hiring for skills is what is changing the relationship between college and the workplace.[8]

Employers still come to college campuses to hire graduates, but because they no longer fill their ranks through promotion from within, the demand for entry-level recruits, who formed the base of the pyramid, is not nearly so great. When employers hire new grads, potential is not the key attribute because they aren't necessarily expecting to grow those graduates into executives. The number of companies like Procter and Gamble that still plan to grow a substantial amount of their talent from entry-level hires has dwindled to a handful.

What employers want from college graduates now is the same thing they want from applicants who have been out of school for years, and that is job skills and the ability to contribute now. That change is fundamental, and it is the reason that getting a good job out of college is now such a challenge.

Even though our Yale graduate of a century ago would feel comfortable at Yale today, higher education as a whole has changed,

TABLE 1.1 Postsecondary Degrees Awarded, 1970–1971 to 2010–2011, Selected Years

Year	Certificates	Associate Degrees	Bachelor's Degrees	Master's Degrees	Doctoral Degrees
1970–1971	—	252,311	839,730	235,564	64,998
1980–1981	—	416,377	935,140	302,637	98,016
1990–1991	—	481,720	1,094,538	342,863	105,547
2000–2001	552,503	578,865	1,244,171	473,502	119,585
2005–2006	715,401	713,066	1,485,242	599,731	138,056
2010–2011	1,029,557	942,327	1,715,913	730,635	163,765

Source: College Board, *How College Shapes Lives 2013*.

especially in the period since the 1970s, in ways that contributed to the breakdown of the pipeline model. One of the important changes has been the rise of alternative forms of further education. Certificates, which are less restrictive than academic degrees and are focused on vocational topics, have exploded in importance. The number of certificates issued by colleges each year now far exceeds the number of two-year degrees. If we included certificates of skills and knowledge issued by industry associations or companies like Microsoft for knowledge about their own systems, certificates dwarf the number of degrees. These certificates are something of a substitute for academic degrees in that they are proof of job skills.

On the college side, bachelor's degrees have also increased in number, doubling since the early 1970s (see Table 1.1). But that increase pales in comparison to the rise of two-year associate degrees. Those degrees tend to be much more vocational than four-year degrees. At the other end of the spectrum, master's degrees have also increased far faster than bachelor's degrees, and master's degrees are even more likely than bachelor's degrees to be focused on jobs. One in three master's degrees now are in business, and many of those are highly focused on the workplace, such as "dispute resolution" or "electronic business technologies."

One of the reasons that associate degree programs are booming is because the United States has cut back substantially on vocational education in high school. Especially for smaller employers, an important source of workers who had at least basic trade skills had been vocational education programs. The number of vocational courses taken has declined precipitously since 1990. Within overall vocational education, industrial arts, which includes skilled trades and other mechanical skills, declined even faster. The average number of credits taken per student in that subject area fell by 50 percent from 2000 to 2005, and the United States already had the least proportion of vocational education in secondary school education of any of the industrialized countries.

Apprenticeship programs have also declined, in large part because the unions, which ran many of these programs, have themselves faded. The Department of Labor data on apprentice programs show a sharp decline from 2002 to 2012 (from roughly 33,000 programs to roughly 21,000) and an even steeper decline in the number of apprentices (from roughly 500,000 in 2003 to approximately 280,000 in 2012). The approximately 50,000 annual graduates of these programs is a drop in the bucket of a labor force of 160 million.

The punch line? If you want the skills to become an electrician today or in fact almost any other kind of hands-on occupation, you probably have to go to college to get them. And unlike vocational education or apprenticeship programs, you have to pay for those skills yourself, up front, before the training begins. The main beneficiaries of this shift have been for-profit colleges, which have targeted precisely this niche for their programs.

Even if we exclude the students in "college" just to get a certificate rather than a degree, the proportion of young people in college is also up. In 2006, 37 percent of individuals age eighteen to twenty-four were in some form of degree-granting program. By 2012, that figure had increased to 41 percent. As a percentage of recent high school graduates, 70 percent were in college in 2009, the highest amount in U.S. history.[9] How this translates into graduates is a more difficult question that I address later, along with how these figures compare to other countries.

Where students are getting their education has also changed. Almost half of college students in 1970 attended state colleges and universities. By 2010, that figure was down to 39 percent. Private colleges have also diminished in importance, falling from 24 percent of college students to 18 percent over the same period. What has taken their place? For-profit colleges, which barely existed forty years ago, now teach over 10 percent of all college students. And, as noted earlier, two-year colleges, especially community colleges, have expanded a lot. Going to college now is much less likely to mean four years on a leafy campus and much more likely to mean occasional classes somewhere in an office complex.

For those who still go to traditional four-year colleges, the path in to and out of them has changed. The idea that we stay with a college and graduate four years later is now pretty unusual. Almost half of students finishing college by the 1990s appear to have attended more than one college,[10] and every indication is that the number has risen since then. When they transfer across colleges, the consequences for the job market are significant. It does help to transfer to a better school but not as much as if the student had been at that school the entire time. We seem to carry the baggage of our first college with us, good or bad.

Probably the biggest source of concern about college now and something of special importance to those who are paying for it has been the decline in graduation rates. Less than 40 percent of full-time students entering four-year colleges in recent years have been graduating in four years. The percentage of students who graduate in six years is surprisingly low as well, less than 60 percent. Those six-year figures are slightly better for private schools (65 percent) and considerably worse at for-profit colleges (42 percent).[11] For those who are skeptical that college won't pay off, here's one basic concern: It's hard to get a return from going to college if you don't finish college, and a lot of people don't. For those who are sure that their kids will graduate in four years or else, I can say from personal experience that demanding that your kids will do so doesn't guarantee that they will. It's not always within their control, as we will see later.

Some part of the overall decline in graduating on time is related to costs. Two-thirds of college students now report that they are working during college.[12] The 1970s began a period of declining incomes for middle- and lower-class Americans, which combined with the rising costs of college to make it very hard to pay for college educations. Sixty-two percent of college students now report that they are working at a job while attending college, and almost 40 percent report that they have what we would think of as a full-time job—more than thirty-five hours per week.[13] Many other students alternate between working full-time and then going to school, picking up a few courses at a time.

Because there are so many part-time students, it is hard to know who has dropped out and who is just on a much longer track. The ability to always go back to school and to complete college over a period of decades if necessary is one of the unique attractions of the U.S. model and a contrast to most countries, where education is assumed to be a full-time activity completed soon after secondary school. You either do it then, or you lose your chance to get into the system, and if you drop out, you are probably through.

Many traditional, four-year colleges have special programs for part-time students, but they are not treated the same way as full-time graduates. Harvard, for example, is said to have more graduates from its part-time bachelor's program than from its famous full-time program. When those part-timers finish college, many of them are likely to go back to wherever they were working because they do not have access to the same job market as do full-time grads. Part-time programs like these may not be a real substitute for full-time college, but they may be the only option for many people.

For students who go to college full-time, the path to graduation now is no longer so certain. The difficulty in securing the classes needed to complete narrower majors often causes delays in completing degree programs. All the new, innovative majors and programs that offer experiences elsewhere or across parts of the campus add a lot of complexity to the system, and as my colleague Robert Zemsky has noted, complexity makes the delivery of those programs unreliable.[14] A joint engineering-biology major sounds great until we find out that the one remaining course in engineering that fits the major is full because engineering-degree students get priority. Spending a year abroad often means having to negotiate which courses taken at another college will be approved for credit at your own college. Unpaid internship opportunities create the same problem—will my college give me academic credit for them? If you are thinking about the economic return from a college degree, the longer it takes to get that degree, the more expensive it becomes and the less time there is to earn a payback from it.

Completion rates began to decline decades ago and worsened between 1972 and 1992, especially for men and especially at the less selective schools. Some part of the decline may have to do with the incoming students being less prepared than in the past, no doubt because so many students are going to college now who would not have applied or been admitted before. But some part of it seems to be attributable to things going on in those less selective colleges and the poorer quality of the experience there.[15] Completion rates improved considerably by 2011—perhaps the bad job market kept more students in school during the Great Recession or kept the more marginal students out—but they are still surprisingly low.

Calculating the Odds of Graduating

The Higher Education Research Institute at UCLA has been tracking the experience of college freshmen across the country for decades. It used that data to produce a calculator that estimates the probability that an entering class or even an individual student attending a four-year college full-time will graduate in four years, in five years, and in six years. The calculation is based on sex, race, high school grades, and SAT or ACT test scores. The results are sobering. Try it yourself at http://www.heri.ucla.edu/GradRateCalculator.php.

One of the reasons that at least some students don't complete college is because they aren't prepared academically for the demands of college classes. In 2000, about 26 percent of first-year students in degree programs in the United States were taking remedial classes designed to cover material that should have been learned in high school. That figure dropped to about 20 percent in 2008, which certainly seems like progress, but we shouldn't be so sure that this decline in course taking reflects a real decline in the need for those courses. The reason to be skeptical of that claim is that most all of the decline came in public institutions, where political pressures and cost containment in general may well have led to fewer of these courses rather than any decline in need.[16]

Another change in the pipeline model has to do with college admissions. Is it more difficult to get into college now than in the past? It certainly seems that way given all the anxiety around college applications, at least for middle-class families. It is true that it is much more difficult to get into some elite schools, in part because so many students from other countries are admitted as well. For them, the competition is indeed worldwide now (see Figure 1.1).

It is therefore surprising to know that half of all the college-degree programs in the United States actually have open admissions: They will take anyone with a high school degree or the equivalent. It's true that most of those schools are two-year colleges, but a quarter of four-year colleges have open admissions. If we think of programs that are even modestly selective—admitting half their applicants—only 10 percent of colleges fit that description.[17] Because most students interested in four-year colleges apply to several of them, a 50 percent acceptance rate is not very picky. In fact, one estimate suggests that about 80 percent of students who apply to the most selective colleges get into at least one of them.[18]

In fact, a common practice now in higher education is to use paid agents to find more applicants and ultimately more student admissions. The agents are paid a commission—think of it as a bounty—for each student they deliver to the college who is then admitted. The practice is most common in foreign countries where the colleges in question do not have any offices or any real recognition, but it exists in the United States as well.

Nor is the hunt for students such a new thing. The ad from Columbia in the 1800s that is shown in Figure 1.2 was part of the common practice of drumming up a student body, up to the last minute before classes began.

FIGURE 1.1. The Campus Crunch

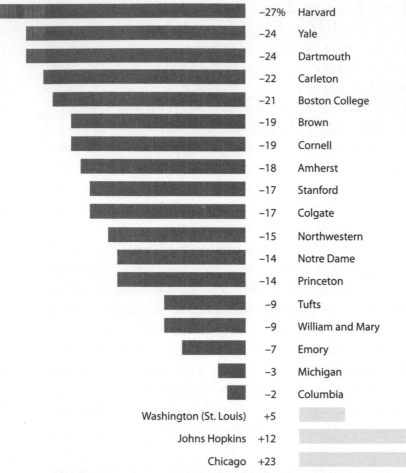

−27%	Harvard
−24	Yale
−24	Dartmouth
−22	Carleton
−21	Boston College
−19	Brown
−19	Cornell
−18	Amherst
−17	Stanford
−17	Colgate
−15	Northwestern
−14	Notre Dame
−14	Princeton
−9	Tufts
−9	William and Mary
−7	Emory
−3	Michigan
−2	Columbia
Washington (St. Louis)	+5
Johns Hopkins	+12
Chicago	+23

Percentage change from 1994 to 2012 in the number of spots for American students at each college, per every 100,000 Americans aged 18 to 21.

Notes: As selective colleges have increased the number of foreign students in the last two decades, slots for Americans have dropped, even as the population of college-age Americans has risen.

Figures adjusted for the size of the college-age population.

Source: David Leonhardt, "Getting into the Ivy's," *New York Times*, April 27, 2014.

A surprising fact about college admissions to four-year colleges in earlier periods was how local the experience was, with the average student going to school within twenty-five miles of his or her home. That changed dramatically with expanding financial aid and with more aggressive college marketing and the willingness of colleges to pursue students far from their own campuses, even using financial aid

FIGURE 1.2. Ivy League Ad for Students

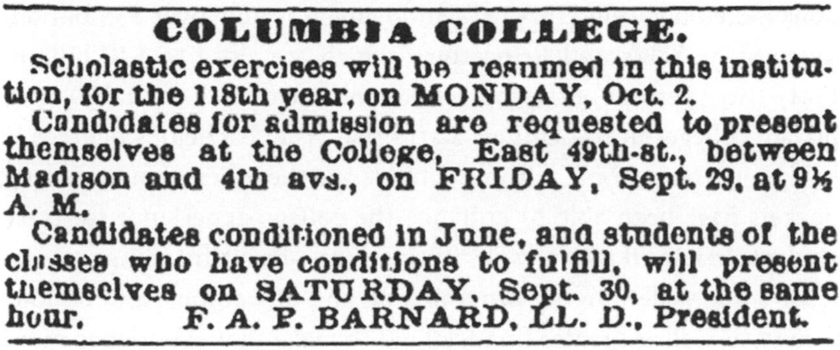

COLUMBIA COLLEGE.

Scholastic exercises will be resumed in this institution, for the 118th year, on MONDAY, Oct. 2.

Candidates for admission are requested to present themselves at the College, East 49th-st., between Madison and 4th avs., on FRIDAY, Sept. 29, at 9½ A. M.

Candidates conditioned in June, and students of the classes who have conditions to fulfill, will present themselves on SATURDAY, Sept. 30, at the same hour.   F. A. P. BARNARD, LL. D., President.

Source: Alison Leigh Cowan, "Remembering When College Was a Buyer's Bazaar," *New York Times*, March 31, 2011.

based on students' abilities to go get them. At my own campus of the University of Pennsylvania, for example, the student body in the 1970s and 1980s was predominantly from the East Coast, especially New York, New Jersey, and Pennsylvania. By the 1990s, the state sending the most applicants to Penn was California.

Marketing has tilted the balance of applications across colleges as well. While there are 2 million more students in college now compared to twenty years ago and the number of four-year colleges is roughly the same, Caroline Hoxby at Stanford calculates that about half the colleges in the United States are actually less selective than fifty years ago. But the top 10 percent of colleges in terms of selectivity have gotten much more difficult to get into not just because of more international applications but because more U.S. students know about and are interested in going to the well-marketed colleges with famous brand names.[19] In the past, many more capable students would have attended a regional college. Average SAT scores at some of these selective colleges, for example, are 20 percent higher than they were a generation ago despite the fact that average scores in the United States have barely changed.

The change in which schools are the most selective tracks changes in the relative fortunes of colleges, in some ways literally so. Since the stock-market recovery in the 1980s and the boom years for investments in the 1990s, the private colleges that started out with money have done incredibly well. Harvard's endowment is now over $35 billion, followed by Yale's and Princeton's, which are close to $20 billion. Forty-three percent of the total endowment across all the 1,300 or so private colleges in the United States that issue bachelor's degrees is held by just ten schools.[20] Those schools and the others that have deep pockets have been able to enhance the college experience for their students in important and substantial ways—beautiful campuses, extensive and wide-ranging programs on and off campus, and famous faculty, as well as greater financial aid to make that experience more affordable.

On the other side of the ledger, public universities that dominated higher education in the 1960s and 1970s, flush with resources then, have been squeezed by declining support from their states. Their attractiveness faded in part because of sharp increases in tuition to help offset the cuts in government aid and because their private-sector peers are doing so much better.

Student Choices

One of the myths about college is that college students today just aren't going into the fields where the jobs are, that they are lingering in liberal arts programs and in majors that don't have any counterparts in the job market. There are places where this is happening. In Italy, for example, graduates with college degrees are more likely to be unemployed (33.3 percent) than are those with a high school degree or even fewer years of education (30.4 percent). At least part of the explanation has to do with the fact that so many students there still pursue degrees in the humanities and so few are in fields like engineering and economics, where employers prefer to hire.[21]

But that is not the case in the United States. The degrees and majors that students pursue have also changed over time, but contrary to what some pundits have said, they have been doing so to follow the job market. The research evidence indicates that students do move to the majors where wages are higher, and they go where the knowledge required in jobs is growing.[22] Fields like computer science have about twenty times as many majors now as in 1970, as do fields like law enforcement and fire prevention, because that's where the jobs are. Business became the most common major in 1980 and remains so today, accounting for one in five students. Other fields have declined, not just classic liberal arts majors like English and foreign languages but also fields like math and physical sciences. The decline in the latter had a lot to do with the change in government policies; they boomed when the government provided lots of money for sciences and math programs during the Cold War with the Soviet Union and for fields that barely exist now, like military technologies, and declined after the fall of the Soviet Union.

A study of how students chose their college majors finds that a big factor in their choices seems to be what they know about pay in different fields. They do not always know the truth about what the pay is, and of course the market may turn out to be quite different when they graduate, but they are trying to go where they believe the market is. Poor information about the market makes their choices worse. Students also choose based on what they believe they are good at, and that reminds us of some limits on the ability of students to go where the jobs are.[23] Pundits like the columnist Ron Wolff argue that students are simply not majoring in the fields that have the big payoffs like petroleum engineering,[24] but the fact is that students are already trying to do just that. They just can't time the market to anticipate what will be the hot field four years or more in the future.

The mistaken belief that students are just not pursing fields where the jobs are has led state legislatures in places like Florida and Texas to think about somehow pushing more students into majors where employers say they want graduates. The employers aren't promising to hire graduates, of course, and this idea of pushing students toward certain fields assumes that the education system can somehow predict what jobs will be in demand when those students graduate, something that requires being able to forecast the economy accurately as well as business needs within the economy. This has never been government's forte.

The argument that students just need to pick the majors where the jobs are also assumes college students are malleable, that a budding history major could just as easily have been an engineer if only he or she had been guided in that direction. We hear that argument frequently about the importance of STEM degrees—science, technology, engineering, and math—so what is wrong with pushing more students into those fields? Even if it were true that there are more jobs in those fields, the problem is that not all that many students are good at those subjects even if they are interested in them. If they could get through the program, would those promising history majors really be better off as mediocre engineers? When employers say that they want more engineers, are we assuming that they just want people with degrees, or do they want good engineers, ones with real ability like those they are seeing now when students make their own choices? The argument that the history major would be better off learning practical material that is useful in a first job is highly debatable, especially if we are concerned about the experience of that individual after his or her first job.

College makes more demands on our cognitive abilities than most of us will ever see again in our lives, and the nature of those demands varies quite dramatically across fields. The demands accelerate in advanced courses associated with college majors. An advanced undergraduate course in physics or logic or French literature requires some real ability in each area, much like being a graduate student in those fields. It isn't the case that any college student could succeed in any major.

Not every major makes the same demands on our abilities, though, nor does it develop our thinking abilities to the same degree. Practical courses that teach content that an entry-level hire could use are often quite simple in terms of the intellectual demands they make on students. Learning the details of the regulatory framework in health care, for example, may be fundamental to an entry-level job in that field, but it is straightforward memorization of content that will likely be replaced by updated material in a year or so.

Liberal arts is typically the major most derided by proponents of the view that education should teach useful skills, but liberal arts may make the greatest intellectual and learning demands on students of any field. The reason is because its distribution requirements typically mean that students must demonstrate competencies across a variety of very different fields, including technical disciplines like science and math, where the conceptual challenges are not only great but quite different from each other.

To be clear, the idea is not that there will be a big financial payoff to a liberal arts degree. It is that there is no guarantee of a payoff from very practical, work-based degrees either, yet that is all those degrees promise. For liberal arts, the claim is different and seems more accurate, that it will enrich your life and provide lessons that extend beyond any individual job. There are centuries of experience providing support for that notion.

Where Do Faculty Send Their Own Kids?

An interesting study compared the college choices of about 4,700 children of college faculty to those of otherwise similar, nonfaculty parents. Not counting students who attend the college where their faculty parent teaches, the children of faculty head toward more elite institutions, perhaps not surprising, but they are much more likely to attend smaller liberal arts colleges. Maybe faculty know something that the critics of liberal arts don't.[25]

And then there is the issue of costs. The most important change in the college landscape for parents over the past generation has probably been the sharp rise in the costs of attending college, which went up four times faster over the past twenty years or so than the overall cost of living. Stories in the press typically point to the high costs of elite private schools when the price of college is mentioned, but in fact the biggest increases in college costs have come at the state universities. Tuition has risen because funds from state governments have been cut and colleges could raise it, especially at public colleges where costs started out at rock-bottom levels: It was still a bargain compared to the private schools, and applicants and their families were willing to pay the higher tuition. At the more selective schools, tuition increases helped pay for even more attractive facilities and arrangements that attracted even more and better students in the equivalent of a higher-education arms race.

Many people who bemoan the expense of education today like to refer to the example of the city colleges of New York when they charged no tuition and enrollment was open to anyone with a high school diploma. The standards in the classroom were high, and a great many students were pushed out, but the opportunity this arrangement offered for upward mobility was unparalleled. The history of the city colleges' tuition practices was not so straightforward, though. The evening classes, which began in 1909, did charge tuition, although it was certainly modest in contemporary terms. If students did well enough in those classes, they could transfer to the day programs, which were free. The period of free tuition for all students did not begin until 1970, and it lasted only until 1976. Then New York's perilous financial situation led the state to take over the city college and university system and impose its standard tuition and financial aid arrangement.[26]

We have to pay much more for college now than in the past, and as we will see in the next chapter, how we pay for it has also changed, with more students borrowing more money to get through their programs. The rise of student loans changes the payoff from college dramatically. It is no longer simply a question of whether families can afford to send their child to college. Now the question is also whether the graduate's future will be hamstrung by loans if he or she can't get a good enough job to pay them off after graduating.

Why the College Decision Is Much Harder Now

To summarize, while the traditional core of four-year, on-campus college education looks very similar to what it was generations ago, much about the college experience has changed. That traditional core accounts for much less of what typical students experience now. Far more students attend college part-time, a large majority even of full-time students take longer than four years to graduate, many now attend for-profit colleges with highly vocational programs, and some go to two-year colleges to get certificates rather than degrees. There are many more options, many more paths to success but also more ways to fail. Costs are much higher, which means that failure is also much worse. All that makes college a much bigger and riskier decision than at any time in the past.

For many families, college education for their children will be the most expensive investment they ever make. Many families are borrowing against their home and their retirement to pay for it. And this is a high-stakes bet. College prices and financial aid obviously affect how that bet pays off, but these are the most straightforward aspects of the decision. Understanding that most people don't pay the sticker price and that you can't tell what the final price will be without actually applying and being accepted at a school—much like buying a car—is the key and obvious factor there.

Less obvious to most people is the fact that if a student goes to college and doesn't graduate, and many don't, the financial gain associated with college just doesn't happen. The United States has among the worst graduation rates of any country. If students have to stay longer to finish, and only a minority now graduate on time, the return on that investment in college also erodes considerably.

Those outcomes—completion rates and time to degree—are not random. They vary across colleges in ways that we can both measure and anticipate. So they will be crucial in determining whether a particular college degree will pay off.

The other factor that is new has to do with the job market. Here is where there is the most misinformation. Even if students do graduate on time, college degrees are not a predictable guarantee of a good career the way they were a generation or so ago. Despite the exhortations about the need for even more college graduates in the economy, anyone following the news in recent years also knows the stories about the difficulty that college grads have had in finding jobs of any kind, not just good jobs.

Former president Bill Clinton is fond of pointing out the link between skills and high pay—"More and more people with specialized skills are finding good jobs"[27]—and the idea that college is the way to get those specialized skills. While it is true that new graduates in some fields command huge salaries, the only reason those jobs pay off so well is precisely because we couldn't predict years ago that they would be hot, so the supply is temporarily depressed relative to the demand. It's supply and demand. In 2014, the highest paid major by far was petroleum engineering, and many observers mention it as an example of how technical skills pay off. What they don't mention is that petroleum engineering has not always paid off. It has gone boom to bust along with oil prices. It was a bust in the 1980s, when graduates in that field were likely to find themselves waiting tables. Since the fracking boom started late in the first decade of the twenty-first century, enrollments tripled, increasing by 55 percent in just one year between 2011 and 2012. The schools producing the graduates believe—rightly—that the huge surge in supply will crush wages and soon make the field unattractive again.[28]

Employers who say that right now they want students with degrees in this field aren't promising to hire students who go into those fields when they graduate. They understand that they can't time the market in order to know what skills will be hot in four or five years and would never make commitments like that. They want you to make those commitments and to take on that risk.

As we will see in Chapter 4, a big drawback to taking that risk is that what employers want now from college graduates is job skills, and outside of a few fields like petroleum engineering and IT, this has rarely been what college produces.

The big shift in college has been toward degrees and majors that mimic at least in name specific job titles like "music therapy" or "forensic accounting." These fields sound as though they are producing job skills that allow a graduate to step right into a career. Whether employers actually value whatever those students learn is an open question, though. Data that might tell us, such as job placement rates, are hard to come by, and what we do know from employers suggests that they don't much care about the academic skills that students have. Perhaps these degrees are just table stakes, a necessary condition to get into the game of finding a job.

A missing piece in the discussion about jobs from college begins with a reminder that all of the focus has been on getting the first job. That first job is truly important, but it is no longer the elevator to a predictable career either. The high-paying first jobs that are hot at the moment in fields like engineering and IT are also notorious for being short-lived. Technologies change quickly, especially in fields like IT, and with it so do skill requirements. The fact that employers can go back to the colleges and hire new graduates to meet those skill needs is precisely why graduates in those fields five years or so out are no longer very valuable. In big companies a generation or so ago, some of that technical talent would transition to management, but now that is rare.

Ask yourself this question: If you were to look around a country club or some other establishment where the successful in midlife congregate, how many of those people would you guess would be working as engineers, biologists, or mathematicians?

One's career is a long-term, perhaps increasingly a lifetime engagement. One of the costs to consider when we pursue courses that are highly practical and potentially attractive to employers in a first job is what we could have been taking instead and how it might be useful later on. After all, the choice does not have to be between learning the reporting requirements of HIPPA (the Health Insurance Portability and Accountability Act) or playing beer pong. We could be taking courses that are less applied but more fundamental, such as how to reason or understand history. There is at least some evidence that the short-run focus on practical course work that might help get the first job has negative consequences for our longer-term career.

Unfortunately, there is no single piece of evidence showing how a college degree will pay off even for a typical student, let alone for the individual ones we care most about. The gap between what the average college grad earns and what the average high school grad earns is often presented as that silver-bullet evidence. Indeed, by some measures, the gap is higher now than it ever has been, and the conventional wisdom is that this proves the payoff. But there are big problems with that conventional wisdom.

The first is the obvious point that what happens on average is much less important than what may happen at the extremes, and in the outcomes from going to college, there are some pretty dramatic extremes. There is a lot of uncertainty in the college game. Some students who graduate from elite schools with very specific majors that are hot when they graduate will do spectacularly well, at least in their first jobs out of college. Others will find themselves in jobs that they would have been doing before they went to college. There is a lot of risk in outcomes, and families are not insurance companies in the business of taking on risk. So higher-risk outcomes are a burden for them. Better information about the factors driving the uncertainty in the payoff from college is therefore very important to help reduce that burden.

The second caveat is that the evidence showing the big payoff from college is more historical than it might seem. The higher income of people with college degrees, which is the main evidence for a payoff, is based on data from individuals who on average have graduated from college decades ago. In fact, that ratio has been quite volatile over time. Perhaps remarkably, college grads in the United States have not always made more money than high school grads, and there is nothing that guarantees that they always will. In those countries where college grads are reluctant to accept jobs that they could have done before college, their labor-market outcomes are actually worse than those of their high-school-grad counterparts.

And simply making more money after getting a degree is not the right test of a payoff because it costs a lot of money to go to college and it takes a lot of time. New college grads would have been more mature and valuable to employers than new high school grads just because they are at least four years older, at a period in their life when those years make a huge difference. The real test is whether the higher wages are enough to offset the investment in time and money associated with college. By that standard, college education does not look nearly as good. In fact, the financial return from attending many colleges actually appears to be *negative*. That's even before we account for the crippling effects that debt taken out to pay for college can have on life after college, especially if a great job never appears. The best thing students could do in such schools to improve the return on their investment is to drop out as soon as they can.

The fact that the outcomes can vary so much across colleges ought to be relevant to everyone. In the rest of the book, I help to pin down what determines that payoff.

The conventional wisdom about college is to go to the most prestigious school that will let you in. Students who graduate from famous schools on average do very well. The evidence suggests, though, that the advice is not so simple. It appears that such elite students might have done very well if they attended a less famous school. Yet it is getting much more difficult to get into the most elite schools, and the tier below them is now substantially easier to get into than in the past.

Colleges in the Middle

Colleges have found themselves in the middle of a dysfunctional supply chain. Employers in industries like IT complain loudly when they don't see enough of the graduates they want, although their specific needs are unpredictable and they aren't promising to hire anyone. Nervous parents on the other side want some guarantee that the investment in their child's education will lead to a good job in the end, again years later, and the days of such guarantees are over. The young college applicants are typically lost in the process. (The informed view at the college end suggests that the best predictor of whether a student applies to a particular college is actually if the weather is nice on the day he or she visits the campus and whether the tour guide is friendly.)

Colleges have responded to the situation in different ways. Their primary interest, though, is to keep their enrollments up, so their main emphasis is to persuade applicants and their parents that they can provide a job at graduation. They have done that with a torrent of very practical and specific degree programs focused on their guess as to what employers want. Colleges themselves are hoping that employers will like these degrees and want to hire students with them.

Consider, for example, the Bakery Science degree program at Kansas State, the Turf and Turfgrass Management programs at Ohio State and Purdue University, Fire Protection Engineering at Oklahoma State and other schools, and Economic Crime Investigation at Utica College. The list goes on indefinitely—remember these are bachelor's degree programs. Drexel University, known for its practical orientation, offers eighty undergraduate majors, but Widner University, a more traditional college near Drexel, offers sixty. Most of these majors sound very sensible—screenwriting, supply chain management, and TV production—because they sound like job titles.

Most colleges are pretty vague about the claim that their practical degree in fields like casino management or health care records administration will actually get your child a job. They let you draw the inference from their marketing. "Each year, thousands of our grads find themselves right where they want to be—employed in their field of study," says DeVry University, for example.[29]

Keeping the Pitch General

This is a pitch from Strayer University: "A bachelor's degree from Strayer University can help provide you with a path to a promotion or a new career. Today, many employers are requiring bachelor's degrees for management-level positions. Our affordable on campus and online undergraduate degrees are all taught with a focus on the skills and knowledge you'll need on the job. And our academic advisors can help you make progress in your chosen field, even before you graduate. Strayer offers bachelor of science degrees in a range of in-demand subject areas: See more at: http://www.strayer.edu/degrees/bachelors #sthash.QY6qPfJW.dpuf."

Being a responsible investor requires some real due diligence to see if that conclusion is true, and that requires getting past the marketing material: Look at the actual data about the jobs that recent grads from that program have gotten, checking to see which employers are showing up to recruit now, and so forth.

For example, DeVry University, one of the most reputable for-profit education providers and one that makes some data on placements readily available, reports that 100 percent of its graduates with communications degrees have jobs related to their field six months after graduation. That figure is based on voluntary reports from graduates, and there were apparently only eight responses from communications majors out of the 8,000 bachelor's degree graduates. The data understandably exclude graduates who failed to look for a job in their field up to six months after graduation. But they also include students who already had jobs in their field before beginning the program, and what counts as "in their field" is not clear.[30] Would you be okay rolling the dice on a degree in communications based on information like that? The National Association of Colleges and Employers, a non-profit research organization, reports that the same year, 6.5 percent of graduates with communications degrees across the country got job offers in their field.[31]

These very specific vocational degrees are not immune from the vagaries of the labor market, of course. In fact, very practical degrees have actually raised the risk level for students considerably. If you graduate in a year when gambling is up and the casinos like your casino management degree, you probably have hit it big. If they aren't hiring when you graduate, you may be even worse off getting a first job with that degree anywhere else precisely because it was so tuned to that group of employers.

An acquaintance decided to pursue a program that would provide the skills to be a court reporter. The program cost over $50,000 and took several years to complete. When the person graduated, the court system had frozen the hiring of new reporters, so there were no jobs. The skills learned really aren't useful elsewhere, and short of moving to a different location, the options are either to wait until new positions open up or write off the investment and do something else.

It's also important to remember that a career is a marathon, not a sprint. Getting a good job right out of college is very important, but if those jobs don't last, the degree may not have bought you much. Graduates with degrees in information technology fields have long known this: IT employers will pay a lot for a graduate with the right programming skills, but those jobs are typically dead ends in terms of careers, and the incumbents either quit or get pushed out after five years or so. This explains why a great many IT grads go into consulting or other fields of business rather than IT per se.

Thinking of a career as a marathon means considering carefully whether what you learn in college will pay off in the long run. Because we only have so much time in college, there is a clear trade-off between course work that is immediately useful in a job—knowing a particular programming language—and course work that pays off over the very long term. Knowing how to distinguish good arguments from bad, understanding human behavior, and having a feel for social changes that truly matter are the skills employers say they really want, especially in the long run.

Why Should College Pay Off?

So far, the assumption has been that college matters because it provides graduates with the skills that are valuable. New students are something like clay, and the college molds them into something useful. The message that it is important to go to college has been pushed from all quarters, in particular, that it is the key to getting ahead. In many speeches to students and parents at high schools, former president Bill Clinton likes to point out that the unemployment rate for college graduates is half what it is for those without a college degree.[32]

There are plenty of caveats to the notion that college educations necessarily pay off, but the fact that college grads earn more on average now than do those who only graduated from high school is unequivocal. Why should that be?

There are two important and quite different frameworks for thinking about the higher wages of college grads. The first is the notion of human capital, that we should think of investments in education broadly defined as similar to investments elsewhere and that investments should on average earn a return. This view has been at the foundation of labor economics for decades; in practice, it is often assumed that education *is* what makes an individual useful on the job. This is essentially the idea that college molds kids into something useful. This view is consistent with the evidence that those who have more education on average have higher earnings.

The second framework is the idea of screening. In higher education, students have to apply, be admitted by the college, and then graduate. Those who can do all that, especially at elite schools, typically have outsize abilities even before they got to college. Some of those abilities have to do with personal attributes, such as perseverance, and others have to do with circumstances, such as particularly supportive families. The better schools both attract and then pick better applicants who come to the campus with more going for them, and that includes wealth and family connections as well as personal attributes. What the school did was identify or prescreen those attributes for employers and others who might grab those students for jobs, marriage, or other associations. Those students most likely would have been successful at any college or indeed even if they had not gone to college.

This view had been associated with sociology, but the idea of screening in other contexts has come to economics as well. It is also consistent with the fact that wages go up with education. It may be particularly relevant for explaining why graduates from elite schools do better than do those in the same field from less selective schools where the curriculum is quite similar.

The best example of screening effects in education comes from the General Educational Development certificate, or GED, the high school equivalency certificate that is based on a standard, nationwide test of academic achievement. The GED test is a one-time, comprehensive test of the accumulated knowledge and skills taught in high school. Many high school graduates would struggle to pass it, especially those who are not college bound. It is not a stretch to say that a student with a GED certificate has the skills and knowledge of those students who stop their education at high school. The GED is just one test, though. It doesn't capture the ability to show up for classes, to get homework done, or to stay out of trouble—at least well enough to avoid getting thrown out before graduation—that is captured in a traditional high school degree.

If academic skills and knowledge were the important factor in a high school education, we would see GED holders do just about as well in the labor market as high school grads do. If the social and personal attributes captured by completing traditional high school are what matters, such as the ability to persevere and get along with others, then those who have GED degrees should do substantially worse. A large body of evidence shows that in fact they do worse, a lot worse.[33] The most likely explanation is that employers care more that students have graduated from high school than whether they simply have the knowledge of a typical high school graduate because being able to graduate from a regular program reveals that you could at least meet the minimum standards of showing up on time, getting some work done, and getting along with other people.

> **Human Capital vs. Screening in the Movies**
>
> The debate between the human capital and the screening view is played out in the bet between the Duke brothers in the movie *Trading Places*. The brothers conspire to switch the life circumstances of Louis Winthorpe III (played by Dan Aykroyd), the Harvard-educated managing director of their investment bank, and Billy Ray Valentine (played by Eddie Murphy), an uneducated street hustler who nevertheless has some real skills. Valentine is placed into a job in the investment company, where the employees are told he is a qualified employee and a college exchange student. Will those credential alone be enough for him to make it in the company? In the meantime, Winthorpe is framed for a crime and fired. Despite his education and other personal attributes, will those negative signals keep him destitute? In the movie, they both end up rich. But it's a movie.

The screening idea says that what employers are primarily interested in when they look at graduates from college as well as from high school are the attributes that came with them to school, such as their native intelligence. A more expansive view of the screening idea is that finishing college reveals lots of desirable things about graduates beyond the academic knowledge they got from their classes, and some of these other desirable skills could have been learned in college. There is a lot of evidence for this view in the reports from employers about what they want in graduates.

Both the human capital and the screening advocates have difficulty in explaining why college educations seem to matter so much after the first job. College graduates, at least traditionally, are still pretty young and don't have a lot of other experiences on which to judge them, so it would not be surprising that their college experiences determine a lot about the first job they get. Why education, and particularly graduating from college, continues to explain differences in wages for individuals decades after they graduate is harder to explain, especially for the advocates of screening. Yes, being able to get through college and graduate does reveal something about being organized and the ability to persevere, but success in your more recent job is far more relevant than what you did in college ten years earlier. It is more credible that college degrees continue to matter because the skills we learn in college continue to be useful in jobs later on, even if not all those skills came from a classroom.

Advocates of the human capital view, which includes most economists, are not home free in their view, though. It taxes our imagination to think that the specific content learned in college classrooms explains success in jobs decades later, especially given how many graduates end up in fields unrelated to their majors. T-shirt aphorisms like the one that says "Another Day and I Haven't Used Algebra Yet" reflect that view, as do studies of experienced workers, like the Center for Creative Learning's surveys of managers, who report that only about 10 percent of the knowledge, skills, and abilities they use on the job were learned in any classroom experience, and that includes formal training. They mostly come from work experience.

The biggest thorn in the side of the view that academic knowledge and skills learned in the classroom determine the payoff from jobs in the future may come from studies of achievement in college as measured by grades and the relationship with performance in jobs. It is certainly true that getting into high-paid professions like law and medicine and indeed any graduate program requires good grades in college. But once in a job, do those who did better in college do better at work?

There are many aspects of college course work that do translate pretty well onto work life after, such as the ability to organize materials, to make presentations, to prepare written arguments, and so forth. Many companies—especially consulting firms—require grades above a given average from college students who want to work for them, presumably because they believe grades measure some of those abilities. Unfortunately, there is no evidence that grades predict much of anything about job performance. Early reviews of the literature found little if any relationship between the two. A more recent review of studies found a modest correlation between grades and job performance, although it appeared to be driven by results from earlier decades and more or less only existed for the first year on the job. The psychologists who conduct virtually all of this research are interested in correlations rather than causation. The overall correlation they found between grades and job performance was 0.16, which might not sound that bad except that it implies that only a little more than 2 percent of the variation in someone's job performance could be predicted by knowing his or her college grades.[34]

Not many employers who require that students have a certain grade point average bother to check to see if that actually predicts who will do well on the job. One that did was Google, and the company concluded that grades predict almost nothing about job performance. So it stopped asking. It also found that its famously quirky interview questions—for example, How many gas stations are in Manhattan?—predicted nothing, so it stopped asking them as well.[35]

There may be something to the law school aphorism that the A students make the professors, the B students make the judges, and the C students make the money. Academic skills and knowledge are most valued in the academic world, which is why doing well in college is necessary to get into graduate schools. Other skills matter more after leaving college. Some of those skills could be learned in college, and some of them might be revealed by being able to graduate from college. The best explanation as to why a college degree seems to matter to wages long after graduation is because that first job after college, when the degree matters most, seems to set the new hire on a career path that determines his or her future earnings. Or at least that was the case historically. Whether that is still true now is an issue I consider shortly.

There is another explanation that explains many of the apparent puzzles in the relationship between college and the labor market, such as why some fields that require lots of education pay little or why jobs in a given field pay so differently over time. That explanation is basic supply and demand. Education pays off when it is in demand and doesn't when it isn't in demand. It pays off when it is scarce and doesn't when it is common. In the 1980s, for example, South Korea embarked on a campaign to increase college enrollments, tripling the number of graduates over a decade. The wage premium associated with going to college fell by half as a result.[36] In the United States, much the same thing happened in the 1970s. More important, the payoff from different majors and fields jumps around in ways that are difficult to anticipate based on changes in the supply of graduates and especially in the demands from business.

Supply and demand explains why a Ph.D. graduate in philosophy earns very little, despite a student's working very hard in school and learning a lot, because the demand for those grads is low. The knowledge itself may be tremendously useful in life and on the job; but the Ph.D. tilts the balance from using the basic lessons of philosophy to "doing" advanced philosophy as a professor, and there aren't that many jobs for professors of philosophy compared to the number of people who would like to do it.

Supply and demand also explains a pattern I describe in more detail later: why graduates in fields like petroleum engineering are in the hottest labor market in the economy right now, while in a different decade, those graduates were waiting tables. It helps to be in a field where demand is hot, but it especially helps to be in that field before other people begin pouring into it. The Hall of Fame baseball player Willie Keeler, one of the best hitters at the turn of the last century, gave famous advice about batting: "Hit 'em where they ain't." That applies to the labor market as well, but it's even harder to execute than in baseball because it requires the ability to anticipate a future you can't yet see: You hit the ball today, and four years or more later, you see where the fielders are.

The fact that students are trying to "hit 'em where they ain't" is precisely one of the reasons why it is so difficult to anticipate which jobs will turn out to be good ones. College students choose majors based on what is hot right now, but they won't graduate for several years. When they do graduate, the new supply would cool off that hot labor market, unless things have already changed, in which case the situation is worse.

Richard Freeman found this happening in the field of engineering. Students shifted into engineering majors when it was hot, but by the time they graduated four years or more later, the field had cooled down. The big supply of new engineers coming into the market then depressed wages and job opportunities. The students in college then shifted their majors to other fields, pushing down the supply of grads in engineering four years later, often when demand had picked up.[37] Much the same thing happened in IT: The recession in 1991 hit IT especially hard, and students in college switched to other fields. That smaller cohort graduated into the mid-1990s IT boom, helping push starting salaries way up. College students saw that and switched into IT, and many of that now much-larger cohort graduated right into the middle of the post-Y2K slump in IT starting in 2001. As wages fell and also as IT work began being outsourced to India, college students moved into other fields, leading to smaller cohorts of graduates later in the first decade of this century.

The lag between picking majors and degrees and the labor market when one graduates is one reason why students should delay choosing their fields until the last minute. It also suggests that employers who are simply expecting that colleges will turn out what they want when they need it are foolish. As in any other field, they need to get closer to their suppliers, in this case the colleges.

Misunderstandings about supply and demand explain some of the apparent frustration of pundits who think the problem with the college job market is simply that kids aren't majoring in the fields where the jobs are. They don't realize that where the jobs are changes over time and also that job openings go away when new candidates start pouring into them.

The market for labor is unlike the very efficient markets we see for something like commodities in other ways as well. People are complex, as are the requirements for most jobs, and education is only a small part of the requirements of any job and of the attributes of any one person. There is enormous variation in the attributes of "college graduates" and in the nature of the jobs they occupy, so talking about average outcomes is not very meaningful if you want to know what will happen to your graduate.

An example of a college labor market that illustrates that college grads don't always do better is China. Despite its booming economy, the unemployment rate of recent college graduates is astonishingly high. Although definitive figures are hard to come by, estimates suggest that 50 percent or more of new grads were unemployed since 2012. We might think this figure indicates an overall shortage of jobs, but unlike in the United States, the unemployment rate for those who are less educated is much lower: Unemployment for college grads age twenty-one to twenty-five is four times greater than for those who only finished elementary school. The jobs available for college grads also pay poorly. Why that is remains something of a puzzle. Most everyone believes there are simply more college grads than there are jobs that require college skills, but unlike in the United States, the college graduates are not willing to take the jobs that less educated workers have.[38]

A fundamental reason why the average results for college grads and the results for any individual may have little to do with each other is the logical problem known as the fallacy of composition: What is true of a group may not necessarily be true of the individuals in that group. Americans may be getting fatter, but that does not mean that every American is getting fatter. Similarly, actions that might be true for an individual might not necessarily be true for all individuals if they all took the same action. Graduates of petroleum engineering programs make a great deal of money right now, but, as we saw earlier, if everyone had a petroleum engineering degree, supply and demand tells us that their wages would plummet. We need to keep this principle in mind in considering the very common policy argument that more people should get more education because it currently pays off for those who have it. Just as our favorite neighborhood restaurant would no longer be so great if everyone discovers it, college and particular college degrees pay off in part because other people don't have them.

A historical example of how education that pays off for an individual no longer pays off when more people have it is the position of clerk. We know from literature in the eighteenth century that the job title of clerk was associated with some prestige. It amounted to reading and writing documents, doing simple sums, and so forth. By the mid-1800s, free public education was established across all the U.S. states, and with it came a dramatic increase in literacy. The job title "clerk" now suggests the very bottom of the white-collar hierarchy of prestige.

Another aspect of real labor markets is that they don't adjust perfectly. At least traditionally, employers have not auctioned off jobs to the lowest bidder. They set job requirements and wages and then look for candidates. One of the consequences of that practice is that the competition among candidates for jobs tends to turn on the attributes of those candidates: Lots of people apply, and we take the one that is most qualified, rather than lowering the wages and other aspects of compensation to the point where the minimally qualified applicants will accept them.

When there are a lot of college graduates relative to the demand for them, as there has been through most of the past decade, many of them cannot get hired into jobs that are perfect matches for their skills because there are lots of candidates who fit the perfect match definition. As a result, those grads apply for jobs that do not require all of their college skills, and when the market is really bad, they apply for jobs that may not use any of those skills.

One of the consequences of this practice is that employers whose jobs only required high-school-level skills find themselves with lots of college applicants in slack times. So they hire the college grads. As a result, the applicants with only high school degrees have to hunt for other jobs, ones that may require less than a high school degree. Some people refer to this process as "bumping," from the practice in seniority-based employment systems in which the most senior worker whose job was cut would then take the job of the next senior worker, bumping that person down to take the job of the next senior worker below him or her, and so forth.

College graduates get jobs out of this process, although not the jobs they necessarily wanted. The high school grads and dropouts end up with even lower-level jobs or more likely no jobs when there is not enough work to go around. The unemployment rate for college grads is lower than that for high school grads as a result, typically about half as much. But that should not be taken as evidence, as it often is, that there are many more jobs that require college degrees. In fact, the opposite is true. The vast majority of current jobs require only a high school degree or less, and the Bureau of Labor Statistics projects that of the new jobs expected between 2012 and 2022, about three times as many will require a high school degree or less than require a bachelor's degree.[39]

The fact that when the labor market is weak, college grads take the jobs that high school grads would otherwise do is a reminder that there is almost always competition for jobs. There are winners and losers in the labor market at all levels. Even in the worst of times, the very best candidates will get jobs—hence the career advice from the comedian Steve Martin: "Be so good they can't ignore you." If you can be that one in one hundred candidate, you are all set in virtually any field. What about the other ninety-nine? Career advice we commonly hear given to young people, that they should follow their passion and they will be fine even in highly competitive fields, makes sense if we believe their passion allows them to be that one in one hundred—or maybe one in 1,000 if the passion is something like poetry or visual arts. But we shouldn't kid ourselves that passion alone is going to work out for the rest of them.

Is what we are seeing from employers temporary? Sustained economic growth might alter these developments. We went from a terrible market for new college grads in the 1970s to a booming market for them in the late 1990s, and the same may happen again. But it will take time. There are still so many people out of work who would come back into the job market if the economy improved and so many who are currently overeducated for the positions they hold that it would take a very long period of economic growth to make the labor markets tight enough so that new graduates will routinely get good jobs.

Even then, there is little reason to think that employers will return to the old days of growing most of their talent from within, hiring for potential and then developing new candidates into lifetime employees. It will take a sea change in how employers think about talent to alter the current equation.

Certainly there are people wealthy enough that the cost of college is not a major consideration for them, but that is a small percentage of the population now in part because wealthier families not eligible for financial aid are paying the ever-higher sticker price of colleges. Even those families are concerned about the careers of their children after college. And everyone should be concerned about this new environment where college appears to be necessary for a child's future, increasingly expensive, but also increasingly risky in terms of career prospects.

So What Do We Do?

It helps to understand something about the business world, the college world, and how they come together to figure out how to get the best return on the investment in a college degree. It also helps to understand that figuring that out is an exercise in risk management. We can't know everything in advance about the job market, but we do know about costs and the factors that influence those costs. We also know something about the factors that make degrees risky. Kids who are about to become college students and then job seekers are really not in a good position to bear a lot of financial risk. Big loans taken out to pay for an education can be crippling if a good job doesn't materialize. Some of these kids are lucky enough to have parents with resources to turn to for help if things don't work out, but few parents have enough resources to bear the costs of an investment in college that does not work out.

When thinking about investments and the return on investments, costs obviously matter. The fact that college costs have soared while incomes have stagnated is one of the reasons why there is and should be so much interest in the payoff from college. Going to a cheaper college certainly makes for a better return on the college investment, but it is very difficult to know for all but the wealthiest families what the actual cost of college will be because financial aid packages are now so much more extensive. The average family applying for financial aid now earns more than $100,000 per year. Many people who could get aid never apply because they think they are not eligible, which of course is a mistake. Getting turned down might be unpleasant, but the benefits of getting aid are surely worth a lot.

Financial aid applications are complicated, though. If you have someone else do your own taxes, that expert can fill out the forms for you quickly. While there is a lot of advice about how to "game" these applications, remember that for parents, cheating on them is a crime, and it could also lead to the student being expelled from college.

There are other types of aid, not based on need, that don't require those applications. Athletic scholarships are the best known, but they are so rare and come with so many strings that they are certainly not something to count on for any applicant. And while there are lots of stories about someone's child who got a scholarship for something strange—yes, there is a scholarship for *Star Trek* fans, but there is only one per year, and it's only for $500—most of those stories are urban myths.[40] For example, while it is true that many schools have chess teams, only a handful offer any financial aid because a student is good at chess. Your children are not going to checkmate their way into the college of their dreams.

The one type of aid that is new in recent years and has become quite prominent is merit aid, basically scholarships for smart kids. Merit-based aid is driven by the fact that many colleges want to attract better students than their current crop. They calculate that if they cut the price of college for certain of those better applicants, they can get them to come. Should a student effectively trade down and take a scholarship at a less selective school than he or she was admitted to elsewhere? If we are thinking just about the return on the investment, this question is certainly worth thinking through carefully, especially if doing so allows the student to avoid burdensome loans or the family to avoid being hobbled in some other way. I consider the evidence later as to whether a more elite school will necessarily pay off.

The biggest cost associated with going to college, though, is likely to be the risk that a student does not graduate on time or, worse, drops out altogether. There is virtually no payoff from college if you don't graduate. Taking an extra year to graduate may well wipe out the cost savings that come from going to a cheaper college. Again, even if we are sure that it won't happen to our child, the fact that a majority of kids do not graduate in four years should wake us up to the idea that our kid might not graduate on time, and making the choices that help them do so is worth it.

Those risks—whether students will drop out, whether they will finish on time—are ones we can do something about. The beauty of the American system of higher education is its fluidity. It is possible to go to college at any age, to start college now and finish years later. One is never out of the opportunity to go to college. If parents have doubts that their child is ready for college, having the child wait another year or so does not mean that he or she cannot go to college, and the likelihood of success there is only improved if that child does wait. A huge proportion of students attend more than one college before they graduate, piecing together a degree along the way and often taking many years to do so. Especially at the state schools, transferring credits from your hometown campus, where you might have started out, to the flagship residential school, where you spent a couple of years, to a college in another city, where you finally graduated after taking a job there, is not that difficult.

There are also aspects of college that affect the likelihood of dropping out and the probability of graduating on time. One of them is the type of support services that are available for students who have trouble. It only takes one serious crisis to throw an otherwise together student off the track and make him or her miss a year or even leave college altogether. Checking on the graduation rate from a college and on the support services for struggling students is relatively easy to do. One of the most common reasons for delays in graduating is the difficulty that students have in getting all the necessary courses to complete majors, especially if they change their major. Figuring out how likely that problem will be is a little tricky, but a good predictor is to see how complicated the majors are—how many of the required courses have to be taken in a particular sequence, how often are the courses offered, and so forth.

Getting our hands around the costs is actually the easier part. Trying to guess which jobs will be hot when the student graduates is next to impossible because the employers themselves don't know. The more focused the program is on particular jobs and industries, the greater the risk. A simple way to assess that risk is to ask what happens if the targeted jobs and employers don't happen to be hiring at graduation, perhaps because their market is down or because skill needs have changed. What do the next-best options look like? If they aren't very good, then you're taking on a great deal of risk.

One way to reduce the risk of being out of sync with the market is to delay commitments to investments in specific skills as long as possible so that the time lag between learning what skills are hot and getting those skills is as short as possible. Waiting to take the most practical courses until just before going on the job market is one way to do that, as is delaying the choice of major until the last minute. Using this approach does require being at a college where changing majors is not that difficult and where getting topical courses is easier, something I discuss later.

This approach is an important reminder that the major may not be the only indicator that matters to employers even in assessing job skills. Take, for example, the field of IT, where we often hear that there are not enough graduates. Most IT work is currently being done by people without IT degrees, and very little of it actually requires a computer science degree from an engineering school, although those who argue that there aren't enough of those graduates don't acknowledge that. A great many college courses now contain a lot of computer work—not just using software but in many cases having to do programming. Having taken a course in the latest hot programming language may make you just as employable as someone with a run-of-the-mill IT major. Being able to demonstrate to employers what material you have learned, no matter what the transcript says, is very important to getting a job. As we will see in Chapter 4, being able to demonstrate skills without necessarily having a practical degree in that field may be the best way to handle the college-to-work challenge.

If the job market in one's field just happens to be very depressed near graduation, the idea of just putting off graduation in hopes of a better job market next year is not crazy. Employers who do extensive hiring at colleges tend to do so in a pretty bureaucratic way, and when they are recruiting this year, they are unlikely to look at students who graduated the previous year. But if last year's student did not officially graduate—staying around to work in a lab and maybe only paying tuition for one course—he or she is eligible for this year's recruiting. It is expensive and possibly unpleasant for students to stay around campus the year after they should have graduated, but it is more unpleasant to have them at home unemployed and sleeping on their parents' couch. Graduating in a down market leaves a negative mark on earnings and career prospects for a decade or more. Taking a job outside your chosen major or one that does not require a college degree at all may well make it more difficult to get into your field of choice than simply waiting out the market and graduating the next year.

There are other costs to pursuing a very focused vocational degree, and those are the lost opportunities, what you could have been learning if you were not in job-focused courses. A class that teaches students the government regulations that apply in a field like health care might be of some interest to an employer, but that knowledge is not going to be useful for long; and the student could have been in classes that provided general, lifelong lessons, such as learning how to make better decisions or to better understand other people. There is evidence I review in later chapters that students who pursued more job-focused educational programs do not do as well in the job market over time as compared to those in more traditional academic programs, even though they may have done better right out of school. A likely explanation is that the job-focused grads were less able to make the transition to jobs that required more than the skills they had after school.

The fact that there is not as much campus hiring in the corporate world now means that much of the hiring that does take place happens informally. Colleges can make that more likely by creating more opportunities for interaction with employers. Co-op programs are the most intensive example, where the classroom experience and temporary job assignments are carefully and tightly linked to show the connections between the two. These programs are widely recognized as effective in helping students prepare for the job market.

The drawback has been that these programs require employers to make commitments to the programs that may go a few years out, and fewer and fewer employers are willing to do that. While a lot of attention is given to co-op programs—they are even ranked by *U.S. News and World Report*—the reality of the programs comes nowhere near the hype. For example, *U.S. News* rates Cornell University as being one of the top-ten schools for co-ops; but co-ops are only available in its engineering school, and there the supply is carefully rationed: Students must apply and be accepted into the co-op experience. The same is true at most colleges.

Internship programs are one of the most common examples of work experience in college, but there are a host of other arrangements for students to interact with employers, some of whom are alumni, through student clubs, charity projects, and class projects. (At Wharton, it is easier to get big-name leaders to come to talk to students than to faculty.) Rural schools are at somewhat of a disadvantage in this regard to the extent that it is difficult for employers to get to the students, but a college that makes a real effort can offset that disadvantage. On-campus recruiting is still important, of course. Rather than taking the college's word as to how good it is at it, go to the career office and see which employers are coming to campus to interview and for what jobs.

Aside from timing the market, there are general attributes that employers say they are looking for in college students, and the answer suggests that academic course work is just not as important as we think it is. Surveys from employers say that the most important attributes in their hiring decisions all have to do with the work experience a student has had. They pay very little attention to academics. Employers are much more interested in what students have done outside the classroom—internships, volunteer experiences, even extracurricular programs—than what they've done in the classroom. Certainly there are exceptions for very applied undergraduate fields like accounting or nursing where the academic content is something of a necessary condition, but the employers do not seem all that enamored with the idea that academic knowledge even in a practical field is the real key to a good job.

Experiences outside the classroom may be as or even more important than a very practical degree. A philosophy major who worked for a summer in hospital administration may be more attractive to an employer than a graduate from a hospital administration program without that work experience. Some of those outside experiences may be part of what one gets from college, but they may also be experiences one can gain in other ways.

Parents with good social networks who can get interesting summer jobs for their kids may not have to worry so much about the marketability of the majors their kids choose. There is also a growing industry of vendors now who promise to teach hands-on job skills to new grads as well as to give them the kind of job experience that is top of mind for employers. These factors might very well trump a practical academic degree in terms of getting a first job. The combination of a serious, broad academic degree and practical job experience in the summer, possibly combined with some skill classes taken elsewhere, might allow graduates to get that first job and also have the abilities to succeed in the long run.

What is the punch line? College educations are a huge investment, and a number of factors affect whether that investment pays off in financial terms. There are literally thousands of schools to choose from, and the choices as to whether and when to go, where to go, how to pay for it, and what to do when you get there matter a great deal to the outcome. In the rest of the book, I pull together the evidence from a variety of different fields to help us think through how to make the right decisions.

2

How Are We Doing?

The State of Education in the United States

EVEN IF YOU are just an observer of the college system in the United States, it's important to have some sense of what is happening in it because as a taxpayer, you are paying for it: About 80 percent of college students in the United States are attending public institutions, heavily subsidized by taxpayers, and most of the other students receive aid from the government in other ways. Every industrialized country supports higher education, and there are lots of sensible reasons why. College provides the educated citizens whom employers want to hire and who will eventually be running everything. What happens in college matters, and one part of that is what we are paying for college and what the graduates are getting in return.

A great deal of the success or failure of college students depends on what they show up with when they arrive on campus. Some of that is genetic, such as their health and basic intellectual abilities; some of it comes from their families, not just values and attitudes but support systems; and a big part it comes from what they learned—or failed to learn—in elementary and secondary schools.

It is surprising to many people, especially those who are focused on discussions about education in Washington, DC, to discover that public schools are mainly the preserve of local governments, specifically local school districts. They provide 44 percent of all the funding,

80 percent of that through property taxes, and a fair amount of oversight as to what is taught as well as direction as to how their schools operate. Each state sets out the general standards that schools within that state are supposed to follow and provides funds that often target special programs and poorer school districts. Assessments of how students are doing and how their schools are performing depend largely on their states. There are huge differences in student achievement across states—Mississippi and Massachusetts anchor the extremes— but there are perhaps even bigger differences within each state. Students in the wealthiest communities often score twice as high on achievement tests measuring the knowledge and skills they have learned as compared to those in the poorest districts right next door.

Despite the bashing the federal government often takes from those who are upset with the cost of education or student achievement, its role in elementary and high school education is quite limited. It provides about 12 percent of total funding and directs most of that to supporting special mandates, such as programs for students with learning disabilities.

There has been a steady drumbeat of negative stories about how U.S. students are performing in school. While public opinion surveys routinely show that Americans think their own schools are doing fine, they believe schools in the country as a whole are sinking fast. Is that true?

A lot of the perception of high schools in particular came from a famous study called "A Nation at Risk," published in 1983,[1] which documented for a country that was pretty complacent about its schools that they were in fact doing a lot worse than they had been a generation before. The data in that report stopped in the 1970s, but the common perception is that things continued down after that.

Just how good a job are K–12 schools doing, especially in preparing students for college? Here's where it matters that we have this decentralized system: States use different measures to assess how much students are learning, and those measures aren't really comparable. Some critics suggest that states do this on purpose, because they don't want to be compared to other states, especially if they think they will come out badly in comparison. Much of the initial resistance to the No Child Left Behind program introduced in the first decade of the twenty-first century by the Bush administration was due to its proposed standard and rigorous assessments of student achievement across states.

Right now, the only credible check on performance across the country is the federal government's National Assessment of Educational Progress, a once-a-year test in reading and math that measures the academic capabilities of students who are nine, thirteen, and seventeen years old. The tests go back to 1973, and they show pretty consistent improvement for nine- and thirteen-year-olds, especially in math. For seventeen-year-olds, just before college, the results are pretty flat—no collapse but no improvement either.

If we look at the test scores broken down by racial groups, however, we see strong improvement for whites and especially for blacks and Hispanics, even for seventeen-year-olds. How can it be that the overall gains are flat while the individual components are improving? This is what's known in statistics as an index number problem, where the index, the combined number, moves differently than the components that make it up. Even though the scores of black and Hispanic students are improving rapidly, they are still lower than for white students, and those students' share of the population of all students has been growing. This would be like finding that the average height of college students has been going down even though the height of both male and female college students is going up because women are shorter than men on average, and they are making up a larger share of the college enrollment.

How about all the dropouts? Kids who don't finish high school are in real trouble in the job market, but we've seen improvements here as well. But much improvement depends on what it means to finish high school. If we look at the official dropout rates, the percentage of students out of school without a degree by age twenty-four has fallen by about half since 1990, down to about 7 percent. That's remarkable progress.[2] On the other hand, if we look at completion rates—how many students graduate from high school and do so on time, within four years of starting—the numbers don't look as good. We see an improvement of about four percentage points since 1990. Not very much. What explains the difference?

It's the GED degree. Students are counted as not having dropped out either if they graduate or if they obtain a high school equivalency degree, the GED. Most of the improvement we see in the dropout rate is because more students are getting the GED degree. Having students get a GED is much better than having them drop out, but having them graduate from high school is better than getting a GED. As we saw earlier, the fact that students with GED certificates don't do nearly as well in jobs as those with high school diplomas suggests that employers care a lot about the high school experience beyond the academic knowledge one gains from it.

If we want to point to one factor that keeps average student achievement down in the United States, it is the performance of the worst schools. The best schools in the United States are as good as or better than the best schools anywhere else. The difference is that our worst schools are really bad.

How about compared to other countries? Every news report seems to show U.S. schools failing and our students falling behind those elsewhere. For example, a recent survey of employers and of the general public found the respondents saying that the United States lags behind developing countries like China, India, and Brazil in preparing students for the workforce, a sense that seems to be common. What's really interesting about these responses, as with similar surveys, is that *most of these people responding have no idea what they are talking about.* These other countries have very little in common in their educational systems, and to the extent that we can describe vast and diverse countries like India and China simply, they are nowhere near as good as the United States in preparing students for anything. India is struggling just to achieve the most basic levels of education across its population; China, as noted earlier, has a generation of unemployed college graduates and is trying hard to catch up with decades of underinvestment in postsecondary education; and while Brazil is increasing its spending on education substantially, it is still well below the average developed country on measures of educational inputs and performance.

The most important of the studies that compare student learning across countries, the Trends in Math and Science Study (TIMSS), which began in 1995, and the Programme for International Student Assessment (PISA), which began in 2000, show that the United States is about in the middle of the rankings of other countries on the various measures of student achievement. We've been in roughly the same place for some time. Our students are not doing worse, and there is no evidence from the comparative data that U.S. schools are failing. Student achievement is going up in the United States, but it is going up in other countries as well, which is why our relative performance remains about the same.

Our position in these rankings is usually reported as if it represents a decline, but in the first of the international comparison studies in 1964, the United States came in eleventh out of twelve countries surveyed. There are many more countries in these rankings now—indeed, there are many more countries period—and so being in the middle means a larger number of countries above us. But the differences between the U.S. scores and those of many of the countries above us are so small that they are not statistically significant. A little secret about many of the new stars of these international tests (Singapore, Shanghai, Hong Kong, and South Korea in particular) is that most of the students taking these tests in those countries are also going to "cram schools" right after their public school day ends. It's not the public schools alone that are producing those results. It's what the parents are doing with their kids after school.[3]

We might rethink our willingness to blame schools for skill problems when we see the results of the newest international comparison, which compares workers rather than students around the world. The U.S. scores seventeenth in literacy, twenty-second in numeracy, and fourteenth in problem solving for adults who have been out of school on average for decades, out of twenty-four countries participating, far below average for employees across countries. This poor performance can't be explained by academic preparation in school:

Compared to these workforce results, U.S. students score much higher on similar tests as compared to students in other countries. Something is happening to the reading and numeracy skills of U.S. workers after they leave school that is different from what is happening in other countries, and it's not good. It's hard to know for sure what that is, but there are two leading candidates. The first is that we don't train employees nearly as much as countries elsewhere, and we don't seem to give workers assignments that are likely to challenge them.

How about the idea that the United States is not producing enough college degrees? The absolute number of bachelor's degrees awarded each year has grown a lot, from just under 1.3 million in 2000–2001 to just over 1.7 million in 2010–2011, or 31 percent. Associate degrees increased by even more, from 580,000 in 2000–2001 to 940,000 in 2010–2011, a 62 percent rise versus only an 11 percent increase in population.[4]

Compared to other countries, it is true that the United States does not lead the world in having the highest percentage of college graduates in the population. That's not a new development. We have not had that distinction since reliable comparative data began being collected. The Soviet Union and other communist countries held the front positions (it didn't seem to help their economies). Russia, Canada, Japan, and Israel have a higher percentage of graduates than does the United States.[5]

Where the United States really does not look good in a comparative sense is our graduation rate. Despite recent improvement, the United States is fourth from the bottom of thirty-four countries in the percentage of students who graduate from high school (not counting GED certificates as graduates). Arguably we do worse with college, where we are second from the bottom, with roughly 60 percent of those who enroll graduating. This low position in the college rankings again may reflect the fact that so many U.S. students are part-time and may eventually graduate but are currently counted as not finishing.

We do lead the world in spending per college degree, however. More is spent per college degree in the United States than any other country (not for elementary and high school education, where we are further down the list), about twice as much as the average, and a higher percentage of the total costs are borne by individuals and their families than in most all industrialized countries. Almost two-thirds of college costs in the United States are borne by individuals and their families. Put together the highest total costs and the highest percentage of those costs, and U.S. students pay far more for college than do students in any other country.[6]

Two other comparative statistics are worth mentioning. The United States is almost at the bottom of industrial countries—twenty-fifth out of twenty-seven—in an important measure of upward mobility: the percentage of students whose parents did not go to college who have made it to college. No doubt the fact that so much more of the costs of college have to be borne by individuals here makes it harder for children from less educated families to get to college because those families tend to be poorer.

The other statistic is the amount of education achieved by age cohort. The United States has the fourth-most-educated population among adults, but we are only fourteenth out of thirty-six in the amount of education that younger adults age twenty-five to thirty-four have. (Number one on that list—with a bullet—is South Korea, where 65 percent in that age group have a college degree, versus 48 percent in the United States.) More of that group in the United States may eventually get an education than in most countries, but that increase will not reduce the gap by much.

What do we make of all these comparisons? Students in the United States are doing better—not worse—than a generation ago. U.S. schools may not be doing well enough, but they are not failing. Students in other countries appear to be doing better as well. Does it matter whether U.S. students are doing better or worse than students in other countries? That information might reveal something about the effectiveness of our education system, but as we saw with the Asian countries at the top of the achievement tables, the differences have as much to do with parenting as they do with public policy.

On the college side, the fact that the United States is the outlier on costs ought to give us pause. But college is a different experience in the United States than it is in other countries. A student's morning walk from a college dorm to meet with an adviser on a U.S. campus contrasts sharply with the bus ride from one's parents' house to a lecture hall with four hundred other students for those in most countries. Intramural sports, clubs, and campus activities are nonexistent on most colleges outside the United States, and they all cost money. Yes, it's a lot cheaper there, but the students are getting something quite different outside the United States.

The fact that U.S. families have to pay so much more of the cost of college compared to families elsewhere is a political choice, one that has changed over time as the costs of public education have risen. The increase in family costs has been justified in part by the argument that the financial benefits of college are so great for graduates in the United States that it makes sense that the graduates should pay for most of it themselves. If it turns out that those benefits are not so great, then that justification has a problem. That is another important reason for finding out whether college pays off for the graduate.

The fact that so few students graduate on time in the United States compared to in other countries, despite the greater support systems on many campuses here, is a tougher set of facts to explain. Part of an explanation no doubt is due to the U.S. system of financing education: Many students can't get through on time because they can't get the money. Perhaps we should also question whether we are sending too many kids to college, at least four-year colleges. The amount of remedial education on U.S. campuses reflects the fact that lots of freshmen enter college unprepared academically for college-level course work. About 26 percent of U.S. college students take at least one remedial course.

Does it matter that other countries have a higher proportion of college graduates than the United States and that the gap is widening? There is no evidence that supply creates its own demand here, that a more educated labor force will cause employers to operate more effectively or the economy to function better once we get above basic levels of education (and the United States and other developed economies are far above that level). The labor force we have now is already far overeducated for the jobs we are doing.

Some of the expansion and improvement of education in other countries is surely an inevitable post–World War II catch-up as the countries devastated by that war, which included every industrial country except Sweden and Switzerland, took decades to have the resources to devote to postsecondary education. Most of the change is the result of political choices. Governments elsewhere are investing a lot more in college education proportionately than the United States is willing to do, in part to give more access to those students whose families do not have enough money to pay for it on their own. It is part of social policy, not economic policy.

How about the common complaint that college students in the United States are not taking the right kind of classes, the hard courses that are needed to do well in college or that are somehow more important, say, in math and science? How much is the right amount is hard to say, but U.S. students are taking more math and science classes now, as we can see from Figure 2.1.

FIGURE 2.1. Percentage of High School Graduates Who Completed Selected Mathematics and Science Courses in High School: 1990 and 2009

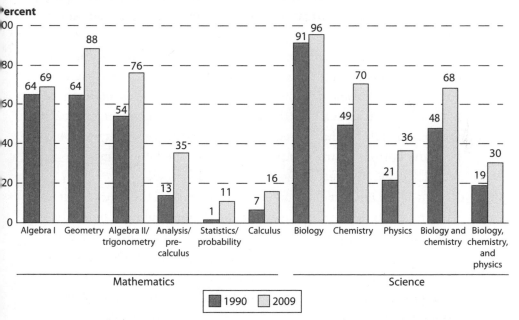

Source: National Center for Education Statistics, "High School Coursetaking," The Condition of Education, last updated February 2014, http://nces.ed.gov/programs/coe/indicator_cod.asp.

One of the biggest concerns in thinking about going to college is what the education options are for high school graduates who do not go on to college. They aren't great. The days when you could leave high school, go down to the plant where your dad worked, and get a job there that might have a future or at least some security are gone. Anyone wanting any kind of decent job after high school needs skills, and the only place to get them now seems to be in some school.

Those of us who went to high school before the 1990s will remember the vocational education programs, where frankly a lot of slower learners were shuttled to learn trade skills that could lead to an immediate job. The fact that those programs were seen as educational dead ends—hard to go on to college from there—made them a target for reformers who were rightly concerned that these programs were in effect putting a ceiling on the career prospects of kids who in many cases already started out with disadvantages. Efforts to reform vocational education included bringing more academic content into the programs and, as a consequence, squeezing out some of the more applied content. In many states and local communities, separate vocational education schools were eliminated, and programs that provided job training were consolidated in the community colleges.[7]

The United States already had the least proportion of vocational education in secondary school education of any of the industrialized countries. Roughly 60 percent of students in Europe leave high school with vocational education training, and while equivalent numbers are not available for the United States, the best guess is that we would be at the bottom of any comparison of developed countries. And in recent decades, the percentage has declined further.

The U.S. Department of Education has tracked the course-taking patterns of students who have graduated from public school since 1990. The biggest area of increase has been in math and science, counter to the common view that students aren't taking these courses. The biggest decline by far—and the drop has been huge—has been in vocational courses or "career and technical education." (See Appendix for data.)

Within vocational education curricula, "industrial arts," which includes skilled trades and other mechanical skills, declined even faster. The average number of credits taken per student in that subject area fell by half from 2000 to 2005.[8] Employers who relied on vocational education to provide their new hires were finding a shrinking pool of candidates. This was especially so for smaller employers: an important source of workers who had at least basic trade skills was vocational education programs in high schools.

At the same time, another important source of job skills for young people declined, and that is apprenticeship programs. Data on the extent of U.S. apprentices and programs is not extensive, but the Department of Labor data on apprentice programs that had registered with it and that met certain quality standards shows a sharp decline from 2002 to 2012 (roughly 33,000 programs to roughly 21,000) and an even steeper decline in the number of apprentices (roughly 500,000 in 2003 to approximately 280,000 in 2012).[9] The approximately 50,000 annual graduates of these programs is a drop in the bucket of a labor force of 160 million.

Whether these measures are representative of trends in all apprenticeship programs is not clear, as there certainly are nonregistered apprenticeship programs, and the data for those other programs is not available in any systematic fashion. The Department of Labor has pushed since 2004 to identify and register more programs, so if the rate of registration has been increasing, then the decline in actual apprentice programs would be greater than the data here suggest. Further, the quality of apprenticeship programs is not necessarily constant either. In the construction industry, for example, union-management joint apprenticeship programs have been in decline as the unions running them have declined. To the extent that there are new programs, they are run typically by individual employers, and the apprentices in these programs do not perform as well as do those in the union-management joint programs, perhaps because the employers are in more of a hurry to get the trainees into the jobs they need now. Many more apprentices leave the employer-led programs before they complete them.

The idea that jobs associated with a vocational track will doom students to low-wage jobs as compared to their college-track peers no longer sounds as plausible now. Unemployed college students are likely to envy the high-wage, outsourcing-proof jobs of craft workers like plumbers.

One of the reasons so many high school graduates now want to go to college is not necessarily because the options associated with college have improved. It is because the options when you don't go have gotten so much worse.

The options are not better for everyone, however. The economists María Prada and Sergio Urzúa found that U.S. students with ability associated with mechanical work but not necessarily strong interpersonal skills or cognitive ability (think IQ scores) were better off in terms of earnings if they did not go to college. These are people who end up as mechanics or machinists or in other high-paid craft jobs. For them, the rate of return for investing in college was actually negative.[10]

Going to college doesn't have to mean going to a four-year college, of course. Two-year colleges, especially for-profit schools, have targeted high school students seeking some kind of skills to get hands-on jobs. Whether what they get is worth the investment is something we will consider later.

Who Are the College Students?

After high school, who goes on to college? A lot of people—almost 70 percent of high school grads, up considerably since 1990 but down a bit since the Great Recession. We also saw a postrecession shift in that more students went to community colleges and fewer went to four-year colleges. Lack of money seems to explain the shift toward the cheaper, shorter option. Many of the high school graduates who do not go to college right after high school may get there eventually, so the long-term numbers may be much higher.

Here's some stunning evidence of how much more time as a population we are spending in higher education now and how we are spending it. The age group of eighteen- to twenty-four-year-olds includes those who left high school at eighteen (or earlier) and started work, those who went to community college and graduated at twenty, and those who graduated at twenty-two under the traditional four-year model, so we wouldn't expect that many to be in college. In 1973, 24 percent of people in this age group were in two-year or four-year colleges. By 2012, the figure was up to 41 percent. The percentage in four-year colleges jumped from 17 percent to its peak of 30 percent in 2011.[11]

Who are the students going on to college from high school? A higher percentage of women than men, by about ten percentage points, go to college from high school. Yes, there is evidence on many campuses of implicit affirmative action for male students, with colleges taking some male applicants with records not as good as comparable women applicants to achieve a better gender balance. More students from wealthier families go—about 52 percent of low-income students versus 82 percent of high-income students. And there are some important differences by race. Hispanic students are now as likely to go to college as are white students, a big change from a generation ago. The stereotype that Asian students all go to college had some truth behind it in the middle of the first decade of this century, when about 90 percent of Asian high school graduates went on to college. That number declined sharply during the Great Recession, perhaps because of the other stereotype: Families making considerable sacrifices to send their children were overwhelmed when the economy went down.

An important concern about who goes to college has to do with remedial education, course work in college that essentially repeats material from high school. This is another reason why the performance of high schools matters to colleges. The amount of time and money spent on remedial education in the late 1990s and first decade of this century was substantial and suggests strongly that a lot of students were not prepared for college. For state governments that are supporting both high schools and colleges, this is a serious waste of resources because they are paying for the same education twice. For private colleges, at a minimum these courses mean that students have to wait longer and have less time to learn the real content associated with colleges. In either situation, it can delay graduation and kill the return on a family's investment in college.

In 2000, 30 percent of students in two-year colleges were taking remedial courses. Perhaps that is not so surprising given that these schools, which are mainly community colleges, are not very selective as to whom they admit. What is a bit of a shock is that 25 percent of students at four-year colleges were also taking remedial courses. In 2008, the percentages fell to 24 percent for two-year colleges and 21 percent for four-year colleges, a move in the right direction and some indication consistent with the idea that secondary schools in the United States may be doing a better job overall.

How Long Do Academic Skills Linger?

A train leaves Chicago for Detroit going 60 mph. At the same time, on an adjacent track, a train leaves Detroit heading for Chicago going 45 mph. Detroit is 280 miles from Chicago. How long will it take until the two trains meet?

Virtually all of us learned how to solve this problem in school—those who were in school more recently did so in elementary school. The fact that most of us can't do it decades or so after learning it doesn't mean we didn't learn it the first time. It means we haven't had occasion to use it again, so we forget it. At least some remedial education may be necessary for students who have been away from high school content for a while. (The answer is 2 hours and 40 minutes.)

The Change in Direction for College Education

Before World War II, college was an experience largely reserved for the elite. Its purpose, which traced its roots back to ancient Greece, was to enlighten students, to teach them the great lessons of Western civilization. When they graduated, they would likely go back into their family businesses or perhaps go into a profession. After World War I, when the GI Bill brought hundreds of thousands of new students to campus and the great state universities began to expand, that elite orientation changed as well. College became something much more utilitarian, and its new mission included providing the employees to run businesses, particularly the giant corporations. Especially for the vast majority of new students, the goal of their education was to help them find a job.

The vocational orientation of education was reflected especially in the rise of engineering programs. Engineers moved from being a reasonably small and somewhat elite profession to making up the bulwark of the management of the leading corporations, virtually all of which were manufacturers.[12]

That vocational orientation maintained a roughly constant trajectory through the 1990s. When service industries like health care and finance began to grow and manufacturing to shrink as proportions of the economy, engineering declined. Degrees in information technology increased, as did those in health care. Business schools expanded in response to the decline in management development programs— basically business skills training—for newly hired bachelor's degree grads in companies.

By the first decade of this century, though, a bigger change was under way that cut across fields and majors, and that was the growing specialization of programs that targeted niches in the job market. In the field of education, for example, it was no longer enough for students to get an education degree. They pursued subspecialty degrees such as special needs education, music therapy, counseling, and so forth targeted to specific jobs in education. It was not so much that the specialized jobs themselves were new. In the past, teachers would move into those roles over time, learning any new skills they needed either on the job or with some training along the way. Now students moved into those jobs directly from graduation.

Every job imaginable has its own degree program now, even sales—Baylor University's Center for Professional Selling teaches students how to be salespeople. Every industry seems to have its own degree program: gaming management, gambling or "gaming" at the University of Nevada, construction management at Drexel University among others, hotel management at many schools, and so forth. And then there are mix-and-match, industry-function hybrids such as casino construction management at Drexel and pharmaceutical marketing at St. Joseph's University.

Nowhere is the vocational emphasis pushed harder than at the for-profit colleges. Their advertisements seem to be everywhere, typically featuring a picture of someone working in a particular job followed by "earn a degree in" a field that contains the name of that job. The advertisements never promise a job, but the implication that the degree in that program from the college in question will lead to a good job is intentional and very strong.

The for-profit colleges have illustrated the perverse financial incentives that the current system of funding education can create for colleges. The schools make money as long as students keep paying tuition, and the surest way to get that tuition is if the students take out loans from the government. The schools probably make even more money if students drop out, as long as they have already paid their tuition, because costs are lower if the students aren't there. And, of course, whether the students actually get jobs when they finish the programs is irrelevant as long as they keep coming in the front end. A flurry of new studies about the for-profit industry suggests, among other things, that they tend to attract poorer students whose parents are less involved in their education, that they seem to do a better job keeping students through graduation, but that the students pay more and have worse job outcomes later on.[13]

The push toward more practical degrees is also on at state schools, where there is no financial incentive to rope students in: State colleges and universities lose money on every student, so more students taking degrees in hospitality management means fewer students in more traditional programs. Here the idea is that practical degrees are somehow more useful to the state because employers like them and the students get jobs, arguments that, as we will see later, may not have evidence to back them up. Perhaps not surprisingly, we see the practical orientation of government-sponsored education debated in other countries as well, and sometimes the push is in the other direction. In India, for example, the higher-education system was set up precisely to focus on job skills (the famous Indian Institutes of Technology, for example). The complaint is that the focus on teaching job skills eroded academic standards, making it difficult to produce well-educated graduates. In Italy, college students have been protesting efforts to direct education more to employer interests, arguing that doing so undermines the long-term interests of the students. Here in the United States, the push toward practical degrees and away from liberal arts has been seen as undermining traditional American values of enhancing individual freedom and autonomy.[14]

Yes, it is true in theory that savvy students could learn which schools are not getting jobs for their graduates and avoid those schools. But for that to happen, the students would need to have hard evidence on actual placement rates. That information at the moment is only available if the schools collect it, which they are unlikely to do if they perceive that the results will look bad. Abuses in the for-profit industry—deceptive advertising, lack of real education and job skills, poor graduation rates, and of course poor job prospects at the end—became so bad that state attorneys general as well as the federal government brought suits for fraud against several for-profit colleges including some of the biggest names. The *Wall Street Journal* reporter Melissa Korn documented the litany of abuses and subsequent lawsuits.[15] The most high-profile attack on these schools came from the comedian John Oliver, whose excoriating description of the industry, led by the claim that one-quarter of its revenue goes into marketing, had more than 2 million views on YouTube the first week after it appeared.[16] In part in response to these exposés, President Obama issued an administrative order protecting veterans (and their government-provided educational benefits) against the most aggressive marketing tactics of the for-profit schools.

How can we tell if there is really any connection between that degree and getting a job in that field, or in any other, for that matter? This is marketing, and a lot of marketing material can be pretty slippery. A typical brochure for a vocational degree program talks generally about hands-on skills, about the practical experience of the instructors, and generally about what goes on in the classroom. What they rarely talk about are job-related outcomes.

The information we'd like to know are things like what kinds of jobs the graduates get immediately after graduation, how much they earn, and where they end up a decade or so later. Schools rarely volunteer that information because it typically doesn't look as good as we'd hope, and so far, there are no national standards that require them to report statistics on job placement. (That is not the case for MBA programs, where accredited schools do report job-placement results in a consistent fashion. The National Association of Colleges and Employers now has a "1st destination survey" that member schools can use to report placements in a standard way, and a reasonable question is to see if the colleges you are considering use it.) For no fault of the schools, some students just don't work out in the labor market, some have life-changing events that take them off career paths, and as a result lots of students in even the best programs don't do that well. So the average outcomes don't look that good. Instead, schools typically talk about representative jobs, which are often the best ones any of their students get.

When schools do provide statistics, can you trust them? One of the problems with information on job outcomes is that there is no standard requirement as to what should be reported and how it should be reported. If we are talking about wages, for example, do we count only those who are working in their field and only those who are in full-time jobs, or do we have to count everyone? Law school professors Morgan Cloud and George Shepard took a look at what law schools reported about the employment outcomes of their own graduates and concluded that the reports were so distorted and deceptive as to break the law. Even on as simple a question as what proportion of graduates have jobs, they found that law school graduates in some schools were counted as "employed" even when they had jobs waiting tables or working part-time.[17] If law schools are breaking the law with deceptive information about their graduates, you can be sure it is happening elsewhere as well.

The federal government has proposed regulations that will require colleges to report evidence about job placement in a standardized manner, but whether that will actually come about and, if it does, when it will be enforced is still an open question. Even colleges that want to collect the information find it difficult to do because it requires following up with graduates who have left the college and who do not have to respond to requests for information on what they are doing. Those who are not doing well are the least likely to respond to the surveys, and many graduates may inflate their own situation in order to make themselves feel better.

The college that may have the most accurate reports on what its graduates do after college is St. Olaf in Minnesota. What it did was simple in principle but hard in practice: It just tracked its graduates down, using online searches, leads from peers, and so forth. For the class of 2011, it caught up with 92 percent of its graduates and found that 64 percent were working and 26 percent were in graduate school. Of course, St. Olaf is pretty open about lots of things, including its own surveys about what its graduates say about the place. What last year's grads said about the jobs they got is shown in Figure 2.2, information that is especially useful if you'd like to

FIGURE 2.2. Financial Independence

y First Paying Job After Graduation

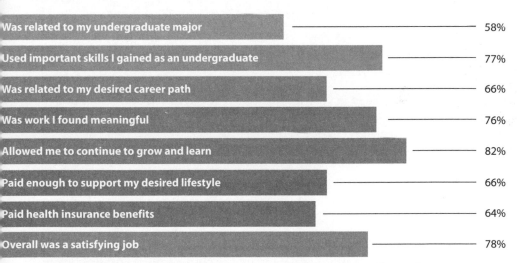

Was related to my undergraduate major	58%
Used important skills I gained as an undergraduate	77%
Was related to my desired career path	66%
Was work I found meaningful	76%
Allowed me to continue to grow and learn	82%
Paid enough to support my desired lifestyle	66%
Paid health insurance benefits	64%
Overall was a satisfying job	78%

Source: Higher Education Data Sharing Consortium (HEDS) Alumni Survey: Classes of 2007–2010 (July 2012).

know what happens after graduating from a quintessential liberal arts program.

So what can we do to get a sense of whether a particular program will actually help a student get a job? Certainly if a school has no statistics available about placement rates or about the employment situation of its graduates, it's a bad sign. Sometimes colleges have that information but don't publicize it, and the place to find it would be on the career center website of the college.

Read That Guarantee Carefully

Several colleges are addressing the concern that parents and students have about getting a job after graduation by providing guarantees that the graduate will get a job. The idea of a guarantee sounds great, but what does it actually mean? What happens if you don't get a job? Do you actually get your money back? No. The guarantees have lots of caveats. They typically cover only graduates with good grades who have followed all the directions of the career service office, and some require that the students have had internships first. The compensation if you don't find a job doesn't exactly make up for not having a job. Most of the schools just allow you to take more courses. (For examples of these guarantees, see Maryalene LaPonsie, "6 Colleges That Guarantee Jobs with Their Degrees," *Money Talks News*, September 11, 2014, http://www.moneytalksnews.com/6-colleges-that-guarantee-jobs-with -their-degrees/.)

In any case, it is very important to go further than the summary information, which is almost impossible to trust. It's necessary to read the definitions used closely. Does a "placement" mean a real job, or can it include part-time work or internships? How is "in your field" defined? What proportion of graduates are represented in the report? Even if you can find all that out, expect the results to be biased way up because the grads have to report the data themselves, and they rarely report bad things.

Data that are more trustworthy are those coming directly from career services offices at colleges. They may not tell you anything reliable about students who do not find jobs through that office and those who found jobs after graduation, but at least for jobs that were offered and accepted while students were still on campus, few schools are likely to misrepresent the results. Divide the number of respondents on the career services data from the total number of grads who didn't go right on to graduate school to get some sense of how effective the college is in securing jobs for its graduates.

Another way to gather important information is to visit the campus career center and see which companies are interviewing students there and what the jobs are that employers are trying to fill. Do the jobs actually require the skills advertised in the college's marketing materials, or are these positions ones that anyone could do, such as entry-level sales or front-line service roles?

Even better information if you can get it comes directly from the employers. Find the top employers hiring in the field being considered. If it's health care, look to the biggest hospital in the region; if it's chemical engineering, find the headquarters of the nearest chemical manufacturer. If you can find someone there to talk to, ask what he or she thinks of the graduates from the school you are considering. If those employers don't recruit at that school, ask him or her why not.

How to Do Better in College

As noted in Chapter 1, the most obvious factor that kills any return from college is dropping out. Taking longer to graduate is a similar problem, especially when students are trying to go to school full-time. How can we avoid these outcomes? The higher-education community takes this question seriously. Colleges don't want students to drop out (with some exceptions noted shortly) because it hurts their revenue and makes them look bad, especially at the more selective schools: If you had your pick of the best high school applicants, and they don't survive in your college, it reflects badly on you.

When the colleges themselves were asked what helped with their own retention challenges, they offered the following responses, which make a good checklist for sorting out where to go:[18]

- *Freshman seminar/university 101 for credit.* The idea here is to create special classes only for freshman, not just entry-level classes that any student can take, that are small enough so instructors can learn who the students are, find which ones are struggling, and help the freshmen feel some connection to the institution.

- *Tutoring program.* Special help for students who are struggling is something that most all colleges offer, so the differentiator is how good the tutoring is and how easy it is to access. A quick test for families is to visit the tutoring center—if the school has a physical location for it—and see who is there. (Don't bother going in the morning, as few students are awake then.) If it feels pretty empty, that's not a good sign, because every campus has students who need help outside of classes.

- *Advising interventions with selected student populations.* Schools with these programs have figured out which demographic groups have the most difficulty surviving in college and try to give them special support. The simplest advising help is to keep the students from taking courses that will be over their heads or over their abilities, where they are likely to fail. Programs like these for minorities, first-generation college students, and athletes are pretty common.

- *Mandated course placement testing program.* The idea here is a step beyond advising students to avoid taking courses that are over their heads. For example, you have to take a test to see whether you are capable of succeeding in the intermediate French class. This issue may not seem so important—perhaps we think students are always trying to take the easiest classes—but in fact, like most of us, students tend to be over-confident about their abilities, something that easily gets them in trouble.

- *Comprehensive learning assistance center/lab.* These programs are beyond tutoring. They help identify learning deficits and challenges that go beyond what tutoring centers can offer. If you ask about these programs and the school points you to a person as its learning assistance center, it's not a great sign.

More generally, one of the best predictors of dropping out is social support. Does it look as though students in the college are connected to each other and to adults in ways that they do not have to initiate themselves? Are there arrangements where they have to see professors and staff regularly (huge lecture classes are not great in this regard) and they have to interact regularly with the same students (small living centers are much better than big dorms)?

Colleges are getting more sophisticated at using data about their students to head off student problems. It is straightforward already to use cameras to take attendance in class and let professors know who is missing class. Georgia State University used data on prior student success to predict how well a given student is likely to perform in various majors. Arizona State University has a program that flags students who start to get into trouble in courses. Big data solutions like these are likely to be used at big universities, and whether they are a good substitute for a supervisor or faculty member who actually sees you at a small college is another matter. But keeping track of what students are doing is certainly getting easier.[19]

The most difficult attributes to assess that affect the ability of students to finish college and to do so on time are those associated with the students themselves because, as in adult life generally, there are so many ways to get in trouble. Health issues, emotional problems, interpersonal complications all play a role. Here is a short list of factors gleaned from a review of studies on college retention, and as we can imagine, these factors also affect who will do well academically and socially:

- *Academic goals.* What is your level of commitment to obtain a college degree? Do you really want to be in college, or were you happier at home? Do you really care about graduating? Even if everything else is fine, if you aren't motivated to finish on time—guess what?—you probably won't.

- *Achievement motivation.* What is your level of motivation to achieve success? As with everything else, if you don't care about doing well in classes, even if you think you are learning a lot, there is a good chance you will fail many of your courses.
- *Academic self-confidence.* If you go into college or indeed anything thinking that you can't make it, the first little setback will prove to you that you can't, and it's easy to give up.
- *Academic-related skills.* These include time-management skills, study skills, and study habits (taking notes, meeting deadlines, using information resources). Smart kids who leave high school with poor study habits are going to find it difficult to learn them quickly enough in college to do well. (I learned this from personal experience.)
- *General self-concept.* As in general in life, people who don't think they are worth much and lack self-confidence find it more difficult to succeed.
- *Institutional commitment.* Are you happy with the school you're attending? Students at a school where they don't want to be don't do as well there. The exception might be those who have transferring to another school as a goal, so that the motivation to get out of their current situation pushes them to succeed.[20]

Colleges are required to report data on their retention rates, and the aspect of retention that gets the most attention is the retention of freshmen: What percentage of incoming students return for the second year? The top schools in this regard are all elite, private colleges. (At the University of Pennsylvania, for example, almost 98 percent of incoming freshmen return.) Some part of that high retention rate probably comes from the nature of the students these colleges select. Colleges try hard to pick students who have all the attributes to succeed, and the most selective colleges have a much easier time getting those students.

Nevertheless, private colleges also tend to have much more support for the kind of programs that head off the problems students have and that deal with them when they arise. Where do you think all that tuition money goes? A huge proportion of the increase in costs at these schools has gone to counseling programs and administrative staff who address student problems.

Doing Better in the Classroom

What should students do in college that will help them later in the job market? Here is where we confront some trade-offs. There are lots of things that we should want to get out of college beyond simply our first job. That includes developing as a person, establishing friends and relationships, finding lifelong interests, and so forth. Graduates looking back on their college experiences rarely point to time in the career center as being the most important experience.

One of the more puzzling findings about the college experience now is that students seem to be spending much less time studying than they did a generation or so ago. The researchers Philip Babcock and Mindy Marks report that full-time college students in 1961 spent about forty hours per week in class and in studying for their classes. But by 2003, that number was down to twenty-seven hours per week. It could be that the teaching and learning process has become so much more efficient that it does not take as long to learn as it did in the past, but that explanation is probably wishful thinking. Time in classes hasn't changed all that much, so the big declines have come about in time spent studying, which declined by about five hours per week. Other data going back further to the 1920s suggest that the decline in study time since then has been even greater.[21]

No doubt the nature of the students who went to college in the 1920s, before financial aid, and in the 1960s, before the big expansion in public colleges, and in the twenty-first century are quite different. The nature of the colleges they attended is also different. With many more students going to college now, a higher percentage of them are less serious about academics, and perhaps many of the new academic programs are less rigorous than the average program in the past. Still, the change is surprising.

What took up the slack in hours? The good news, especially for those who are paying for college, is that time spent in leisure hasn't changed much. Time spent working in a job while attending college as a full-time student doubled to eight and a half hours per week, and some of that may be related to the expansion of work-study financial aid. We can't be sure what else is taking up eight hours or so, but even a casual comparison of college now to a generation ago indicates that programming outside of class—intramural sports, clubs, community service, and so forth—are far more important than in the past.

We also know from studies within individual schools that time spent hunting for jobs is way up. At elite business schools and colleges that are producing students who are in demand from employers, time spent in recruiting has soared. The paradox here is that because the students are in demand, they spend a great deal of time sorting through the options, especially meeting with employers that are visiting campus. Students' self-reported time spent in job search during the academic year often tops twenty to thirty hours per week. Nor is this time spent just concentrated in what we used to think of as recruiting season, just before graduation. In business schools, the process starts *in the fall of students' first year,* competing for summer jobs. The same process happens in law schools, where the job hunt for crucial summer positions begins in the first year of a three-year program. Job hunting is a bit more diffuse for undergrads, but recruiting for summer jobs happens every year.

One way to describe this situation is that employers are competing so hard to get some students that it disrupts in a serious way the learning experience of those students. On the other hand, students in programs that are less hot for employers are fighting to get any attention from them. While this situation may seem understandable, it is not the way we think a market ought to work.

As we saw earlier, college grades are not a good predictor of success in jobs, although they do drive the increasingly important access to graduate schools and the jobs for which those schools provide entry. We do know some things about what students can do to learn more in college, at least as measured by their grades.

Social scientists have been learning more and more about the effects of peers on our behavior. These effects are especially powerful in college in part because students are typically on their own for the first time and are literally living with other people. One of the first and most influential of the studies of peer effects in college took place at Dartmouth College, where, as in many schools, roommates were as-signed randomly—always a good thing for the purposes of research. The economist Bruce Sacerdote found that students whose room-mates did better in their courses also did better.[22] Follow-on studies confirmed other effects that anyone who has been a freshman in col-lege will recognize, that roommates influence decisions involving risky behavior, such as drug use, and that the student teams created for college programs also create peer effects. The moral here is to be careful who your roommate is. More generally, if you are in a school where everyone is serious about the course work, you are likely to be more serious as well.

One of the worst outcomes from the college experience is to drop out. There are many reasons why doing so is bad, but the effects are clearest in the labor market. A wide range of factors can affect the de-cision to quit college, many of which are beyond the control of the student. The ones that worry us the most, though, are those within the control of the student, such that dropping out could have been prevented. Of these, perhaps the most important has to do with stu-dents' own expectations. Todd and Ralph Stinebrickner found that at least at one college, students who dropped out were inclined to be overly optimistic about their ability. They also found that unreason-able expectations about ability helped explain dropping out of science majors.[23] Studies in psychology tell us that expectations about ability matter in two ways. First, we may not work as hard if we think we have great ability because we think we do not need to, and that causes us to do poorly. Second, many people are inclined to believe that per-formance results more from ability than from effort, so when we learn that our ability is not as great as we think, we may give up.

There is a burgeoning literature on what motivates students to learn, and the short answer seems to be that it is much the same as the things that motivate us to do anything. The rewards and punishments associated with staying in college and doing well there are already pretty great, and most of the studies focus on factors that are easier to manipulate, such as changing the attitudes of students about how much control they have over their performance (more than they think) or setting goals. The evidence suggests that counseling programs to improve students' motivation using these techniques do work. The lesson here is to check out the support programs that colleges have and to pay special attention to those that are sophisticated about improving motivation.

But studying still matters. The evidence suggests that last-minute cramming doesn't work well, regular study time does help, and going over practice questions helps a lot.[24]

Most colleges have tutoring programs and other arrangements to help kids who are struggling in classes, but of course they are not all equally good. Even in the age of online learning, good help still requires skilled staff who can diagnose what's wrong, figure out good solutions, and follow up with the student.

All that costs money.

Virtually all colleges now have mental health counseling and crisis management programs, although again they are not all equally good. The best of the student support services are those that try to head off crises before they happen. That can be a tall order when the incoming class is full of high school valedictorians, and by definition, most of those will not end up at the top of their new class. The stress of students not meeting their expectations—in their own minds and often in those of their parents and families as well—can be almost unbearable.

The Wharton School has a computer-based simulation that walks admitted students through the key decisions and requirements of the first year in college so that they can try out how they would address them and then see what the consequences of those decisions would be before they have to make them for real.[25] Harvard has a program designed to help its students understand what success should mean to them, broadening the view beyond achievement in the form of grades to all aspects of life in college and in the process taking away some of the single-minded focus on grades.[26] Stanford's program focuses specifically on resilience, the importance of being able to handle failure and keep going.[27] The idea in all of these programs is not just to get students through their college years without emotional and related crises but to help them become adults who can also survive the knocks of life after college.

One of the reasons that the expensive, elite colleges have much better graduation rates than even their elite public college peers (think Stanford versus Berkeley) is because the more extensive support services at the former get kids through. These programs of academic support are expensive because they require a lot of trained counselors, which is why not all colleges can offer them. If we are thinking realistically about what students need to succeed in college, programs like these are far more important than are attractive dormitories and fancy gyms. Most people don't want to think that their own child could need special help in college, and no doubt it seems like a rare event to many parents because families whose kids had crises in college don't necessarily talk about it. Planning for college without considering what support services are available, though, is like picking a spot to go mountain climbing without checking to see whether there are rescue services that could get you out if something bad happens.

So far, this discussion has all been about problems that students have that can get in their way of finishing school. Some problems come from the school itself, though, and the most common one is the requirements for particular degrees or particular majors. It is very common for students to find themselves unable to finish a program or at least to finish it on time because the course they need to fulfill the requirements is not being offered or the prerequisites for the course are too difficult to complete.

Why would a college create a situation where students can't get the courses they need to graduate? They don't do it on purpose. It happens because other goals get in the way. Think of this as a supply chain problem: Faculty develop the course list required for majors, and they don't necessarily do it with the goal of making it easy to get through the program. Who is going to teach those required classes is determined later, and that decision is in second place behind what individual faculty are able to teach and want to teach, when they go on leave, and so forth.

How can you tell whether it will be easy or difficult to complete majors? The more complicated the major, the more likely things will go wrong. What makes a major complicated? The more courses required, the more courses that cut across departments and schools, and especially the more prerequisites required for courses in the major (for example, students need these three classes in this order before taking this last course) all make it more likely for something to go wrong that delays finishing the major on time. Having to take courses in a certain order is probably the biggest problem causer because anything that goes wrong with any of the courses in the chain can cause delays.

Will College Get Cheaper?

College in the United States is a very expensive institution. There is no doubt that education could be delivered much less expensively, and there is a lot of discussion now about ways in which that could happen. Whether a similar experience could be delivered at a substantially lower cost is a harder question. For example, in much of the rest of the world, students live with their families while going to college, which certainly cuts down on the cost, but it also eliminates much of the "learning to live on your own" experience that many people see as the greatest value of the U.S. model. We could have bigger classes, hire instructors who teach more and do not spend time doing research, get rid of the support systems that account for much of the recent cost increases, drop the extracurricular activities, shift assignments to multiple-choice tests that can be machine graded, and so forth, all of which could drop the cost of college dramatically.

This is much of the appeal of MOOCs—massive open online courses—that have received a great deal of attention in recent years. The idea started at places like MIT, where faculty were asked to make all their teaching materials available online. In practice, what was posted were PowerPoint slides and handouts, and a look at those early courses shows that it wasn't possible to learn much from them without the classroom experience.

MOOCs, however, are an important step beyond PowerPoint slides and handouts. Here, faculty actually teach courses designed to be delivered online. Lectures are videotaped, and sometimes class discussions with students in the room are made available, along with handouts, slides, and so forth. A student can essentially take the course anywhere that an Internet connection is available, and that seems to many people like a paradigm shift—except for those who knew that arrangements like this have been around for a century. Expert faculty put all their lecture notes along with problems that could be worked through with guidance and correct answers, illustrations, commentary, and more in a single place that students could access anywhere at any time. It was called a textbook. In the 1960s, many cities in the United States had TV programs like *Sunrise Semester,* on which local college professors taught a televised version of the course usually very early in the morning before regular programming began. Unlike virtually all the MOOC programs, students could actually get college credit for *Sunrise Semester* courses. Starting in the 1990s, the same thing was available on CD-ROM.

MOOCs got attention when thousands of potential students, mainly in developing countries, signed up to participate in such courses online. The fact that virtually none of them completed the courses got less attention.

But we certainly could have very inexpensive programs based on MOOCs—or even based on textbooks. We could set up online tests to indicate mastery of the content in MOOCs, and we could give students course credits for passing the tests. In fact, the burgeoning world of skill-based credentials already works exactly like that. Specialized testing companies provide secure facilities to ensure that the test taker is doing his or her own work, and however the material was learned, passing the test leads to the credential.

We could say that a student who passes thirty-two approved tests of that sort based on content associated with college courses gets a college degree. Some schools are already doing this. The University of

Arizona's Outreach College, which offers degrees taught entirely on-line, received a huge boost with the announcement that Starbucks will pay the tuition costs for employees who want to pursue a degree there.[28] Is it the same thing as a regular bachelor's degree from the University of Arizona? Of course not, and so far, the colleges have tried to keep their on-campus brands separate from their online brands. Will it give graduates a big boost in the job market? The evidence we have so far suggests no. Consider the experience described earlier with the GED high school equivalency degree. Despite the fact that it represents at least as good a mastery of academic material as a reg-ular degree does, the payoffs to it are substantially less. The material we saw earlier on employers' interests indicates that they don't care all that much about the academic content of the college experience. They are after precisely the experiences that cannot be taught online.

A survey of employers by the *Chronicle of Higher Education* con-firms that conclusion. They were asked how they viewed various alternatives to a traditional four-year degree. They rated "competency-based" programs, where students can learn on their own and get course credits by passing exams that they can take at any time, as far less desirable than a traditional four-year program. They also rated three-year programs lower, where students either take courses through what are vacation periods in the four-year program or take a program that trims some of the elective courses. (See Appendix for the scores.) Presumably the main difference with a four-year degree is that there is less time to grow up and less time for extracurricular activities. As with the GED degrees, it isn't the mastery of the academic content that seems to matter.

Colleges have been experimenting with cheaper, prepackaged de-livery of course material for decades, such as videotaped lectures or simulations that are incorporated into standard classes. Most colleges do make use of some of this material in some ways. There is no evi-dence to suggest that it is a magic bullet for colleges and especially for learning. Even for-profit education providers like the University of Phoenix learned that entirely online instruction doesn't work particularly well. They built bricks-and-mortar classrooms around the country to deliver much of their educational content the same way most colleges do: smaller classes with instructors in front of the room.

If education gets cheaper to deliver, that doesn't mean the price will come down. Costs and prices aren't the same thing. If college gets cheaper to deliver, the savings might well go into new programs and additional benefits for the community. What schools charge now is not based on costs—remember that tuition doesn't cover the costs in most colleges. So expecting some breakthrough to bring down the cost of college tuition is likely to be disappointing.

The College Market Outside the United States

One very simple way to get a lower-cost education is to leave the United States. Unless you are going to the public colleges and universities in your own state, college educations are cheaper even for foreigners in virtually every country in the world than they are in the United States. At Oxford University, for example, the tuition costs for the famous Politics, Philosophy, and Economics program that many Rhodes Scholars take is about US$25,000 at current exchange rates, an absolute steal compared to the costs of elite schools in the United States, and the degree comes in three years. Of course, you have to be admitted first.

Degrees in Scotland, where the program is four years and looks more like the U.S. model (which in fact was borrowed from Scotland) are considerably cheaper, closer to $15,000 depending on the university and the exchange rate. Nearer home, tuition costs at Canadian colleges and universities are also cheap, priced about like those in the United Kingdom. College can be even cheaper if one is willing to leave English-speaking countries. College is hard enough even for native speakers, though, so it is easy to be overwhelmed by trying to master a new language, manage a new culture, and handle college-level course work.

Why not leave the country? We see so many foreign students coming to the United States for their education; surely the other way around can work as well. One caveat is that we don't see the foreign students who fail. The counseling services at most any college in the United States know the many additional difficulties that students coming from other countries have to overcome just to survive in college here. As we saw earlier, U.S. colleges have lots of support services to help struggling students. These services are much less common outside the United States.

The biggest caveat in going to college outside the United States is the job market after college. If you want a job in Canada after graduation, by all means go to a Canadian college, but if you want a job back in the United States, don't expect any help from your Canadian alma mater. Career services on campus in other countries tend to be far less developed than those in the United States, and to the extent they exist, they focus on their local employers. If you want to go to graduate school after college rather than getting a job, it might be perfectly fine to have a degree from a foreign college, as long as it is respected internationally. But if you want a job after, especially if you want one back in the United States, you're on your own to find it.

There is a great deal of misinformation about education in the United States. Most of our attention is focused on K–12 education, where we are doing better than the popular perception suggests. The bigger challenges may well be at the college level, where we send a great number of students, where we pay a huge amount for that education, and where graduation rates are very poor. We expect college to give graduates access to better jobs, but whether that actually happens is very difficult to assess. What we do know is that there is a great deal of variation across colleges—in what they cost, in what they offer students, and, it would seem, in how good a job they do in helping students get on with their careers. That variation means that the choice of where to go and what to major in—the issue we consider next—are crucially important in determining whether college pays off.

3

Does College Pay Off?

It Depends

Whether going to college pays off is a complicated question because it has many moving parts. It's not that hard to see what college graduates earn, but there is so much variation in what they earn depending on which college they go to, which field they are in, and when they graduate that looking at average figures is really not very helpful for making individual decisions.

The next problem is trying to figure out what the cost is. The value of earning a lot diminishes if it costs a lot to get it, a topic we return to in the next chapter. The hardest question to answer in order to know whether college pays off is, compared to what? As noted in Chapter 1, many kids who go to college are pretty able before they get there. They may have done well later in life even without college. Sorting out how much of their later success is due to college and how much is due to the attributes that would have gotten them into college in the first place is not easy to answer. Some of what happens in college that is valuable is just growing up, which could have occurred even if they had not gone to college.

The final issue, perhaps the most difficult, is trying to get some handle on what the job market will be like in the future. The way the market behaved in the past is no guarantee of the future, of course. Will it be like the roaring 1990s, the period that drives much of the recent evidence of the payoff to college, or will it be like the post-recession period right now, the worst labor market since the Great Depression?

A simple story about the economic benefits of going to college, and the one on which most of the attention is placed, is the "college wage premium," which is how much more the average college graduate in the labor market earns as compared to the average high school graduate. The fact that the two groups on average are likely to hold different jobs is the main factor driving the size of that premium.

The economists Daron Acemoglu and David Autor at MIT calculated the average weekly wages of workers, discounted for inflation over time, by education level—high school dropouts, high school grads, those with some college, college grads, and those with graduate degrees.[1] The most interesting point about the wage gap between those different groups over time is how much it has changed. High school dropouts, high school grads, and college grads made much the same weekly pay in the early 1960s and then again in the mid- to late 1970s. This is hard to believe given contemporary discussions about the great value that college adds to earning power.

Then something happened right after the 1981 recession. Real wages for everyone with less education than a four-year college degree started to collapse. They continued to decline through the early 1990s, especially for high school dropouts. The end of high-paying, union manufacturing and the rise of low-wage competition, from China in particular, is certainly a big part of the explanation. Wages for college grads didn't take off, but they at least recovered. By the end of the 1990s, they were back to where they had been in the early 1970s.

The result of these two movements—the recovery of real wages for college grads, the continued decline for everyone else—created a big gap between the groups and a sizeable wage premium for college graduates. But we should remember that the increased premium was mainly produced by the decline in wages for the noncollege group. Suddenly it paid to have a college degree because the wages if you didn't have one were awful. Just before the Great Recession in 2008, college graduates were earning about 60 percent more than high school graduates. Where the wage premium went during the Great Recession is the subject of some debate, but the U.S. Department of Education calculates that it declined a bit from a peak of 69 percent to 63 percent.

The size of that wage premium is the attention-getting headline that has been used to make the case for more people to go to college. As the columnist David Leonard at the *New York Times* asserted, "The decision not to attend college for fear that it's a bad deal is among the most economically irrational decisions anybody could make in 2014."[2] There are a lot of reasons to be skeptical about that conclusion, however. The first reason is simply that the college wage premium has been a remarkably volatile measure, especially considering that it is calculated as the average of the workforce of 160 million. In the early 1960s and again in the late 1970s, the gap was virtually nonexistent. Given what we've just seen, the idea that it will stay where it is today going forward seems unlikely. It's not just changes in the economy that can alter the college wage premium; it's changes in the number of people going to college. The accepted view of the labor market from the late 1960s through the 1970s was that the influx of these college grads not only kept the wage premium down but was actually a drag on the economy because it introduced so many new workers without job skills.

There is debate on why the college wage premium changed and why it might change again. Political scientists and sociologists are inclined to point to political changes that shifted power to employers and the associated decline in unions, which reduced labor's ability to hold up wages and drove down the wages of high school grads. In other words, the story is really about the collapse of wages for the less educated. Economists are inclined to believe that something about the economy changed that increased the value of education. The reason for that conclusion has to do with supply and demand. In the period from the early 1980s through the early 1990s, the supply of college grads was increasing as compared to the workforce as a whole, in part as the tail of the baby boom entered the workforce and in part because more high school grads went on to college. So if the relative wage for college grads was rising even as the supply of college grads increased, then it must be that the demand for college grads was rising. In other words, it's a story about the demand for college grads.

The question is, what happens in the future? Is the current period an anomaly as well, just like the low premium period of the 1970s? Or is it something permanent?

The arguments suggesting that the premium is up and will stay up come typically from economists, and here is where a quick plunge into that literature is important. The phrase "skill-biased technological change" is used by economists as the explanation as to why the college premium is up and will likely continue to stay up. The assertion is that skill requirements always go up in economies as the result of economic progress and that rising skill requirements increase the demand for college graduates over high school graduates, hence the idea that technological change favors or is biased toward raising skill requirements. Given that assertion, what shapes the wage levels of college grads as opposed to high school grads is simply the relative supply of those two groups.

We know that new technology doesn't always raise skill requirements, of course. The assembly line, for example, was designed precisely to reduce skill requirements for factory jobs. But the rise of information technology and associated jobs in programming, IT systems, and so forth created the sense from the late 1990s on that maybe something about technology was driving wage levels now. And indeed the evidence suggested that just having a job that required using a computer was enough to cause wages to be higher.

The more sophisticated view of technology in the first decade of this century was that information technology creates higher-skill jobs for those who have to build the systems and also lowers skill requirements for those who use the technology. It takes considerable skill to create word-processing software, for example, but using it requires less skill than typists would typically have. This explanation seemed to explain some of the rising inequality in wages through the first decade of the century.

What happened since then confounds the picture further. The Great Recession caused by the financial crisis in 2008 is the defining event of the new millennium, throwing an estimated 300 million people around the globe out of work. The U.S. economy is about 13 percent smaller in 2014 than our best guess as to where it would have been had the Great Recession not taken place. The population is about 13 percent bigger, however, so the per person losses in income are substantial.[3] The costs have not been borne evenly, though. People who lost their jobs obviously lost much more than those who kept their jobs, and those who entered the labor force during the Great Recession have had a much harder time than those who entered before it.

Beyond that, there is some evidence of other, unpleasant developments in the labor market. Some evidence suggests that the number of jobs that demand more cognitive skills has been shrinking. If so, college grads will find less demand for their skills and in turn look to jobs that require fewer skills. In the process, they "bump" the applicants without a college degree, who then end up with even lower-skilled jobs or none at all. There is considerable evidence that a lot of this happened in the Great Recession. As one set of authors put it, "Relative to the 1990s, it is a future where even the demand for skilled workers is reduced. In this maturity stage, having a BA is less about obtaining access to high paying managerial and technology jobs and more about beating out less educated workers for the Barista or clerical job."[4] It's a guess, though, as to where things will go from here.

A second, basic reason for discounting the size of the college wage premium, especially as it is often interpreted, is that, as noted earlier, the average college graduate has advantages before he or she even starts college as compared to the average high school graduate. Those who complete college have also demonstrated some useful abilities that they probably had before going to college, such as the ability to persevere, especially as compared to those who start but do not finish college and end up in the "high school only" wage category.

The assertion about the college wage premium is often that the typical high school graduate would earn what the typical college graduate earns if only he or she had gone to college. That is simply not true. He or she would likely earn considerably less, or put differently, the college grad who had only gone to high school would earn considerably more than the average high school grad because of the greater abilities and advantages he or she had at age eighteen.

Nor is the college wage premium an apples-to-apples comparison over time. In 1981, only 26 percent of people aged eighteen to twenty-four attended four-year colleges, while by 2011, the figure was up to 42 percent. More able high school students went on to college as time went on, so the "high school only" population by definition was less able.[5] Another important caveat is that the GED is now counted as equivalent to a high school degree in most of the calculations of the college premium, although it was not always so, and we know that the wages of GED recipients are well below those of regular high school graduates. Counting in the GED started about the time that the data indicated a big jump in the college wage premium. All those factors make the premium less representative of the experience of typical college graduates.

Perhaps the biggest reason to be cautious about generalizing from the college wage premium is that it is calculated for the labor force as a whole, and the average worker whose experience it represents has been out of school for decades. There is no reason to expect that the premium that new graduates will earn will look like that of the much older and more experienced average worker. Even now we know that the annual wage premium for college graduates age twenty-five to thirty-five is 50 percent in the most recent period, compared to over 60 percent for all those over age twenty-five—higher for workers who have been out of college longer. We would have thought that if college skills were the driving factor in the wage premium, the reverse would be true because the benefits of college per se would begin to wane as work experience becomes more important.

If we look at what has happened to the wages of young workers age twenty-one to twenty-four in the past decade, we learn something about the experience of recent school leavers. It is really a story about which group lost and lost the fastest as both high school and college grads have seen falling real wages since 2002. Wages for college-educated men have been especially volatile, but wages for women college graduates have been hit especially hard. The sex difference is probably explained by the fact that men are disproportionately in manufacturing and construction jobs while women are disproportionately in service jobs. Men's jobs were perhaps more likely to see layoffs, which are not accounted for in wage data as they only include those with jobs, while women's jobs suffered fewer layoffs but apparently more wage cuts.[6]

The college wage premium in the United States is near the top of any country in the world and indeed is higher than that of any other major industrial country (only Chile, Brazil, Hungary, and Slovenia have a higher premium). As noted earlier, in countries like Italy and China, new college grads are having a worse time in the job market than are high school grads. That might give a little pause to the notion that there is something inevitable about the size of the college wage premium in the U.S. experience as it doesn't seem to be playing out the same way in other countries.

The wage premium that college grads earn over high school grads is very important for people who are trying to understand where the economy is going and why. It is not that useful for trying to predict whether a college degree in a few years will pay off in part because the wage premium measures have been so volatile over time, because they are backward looking, being based largely on people who graduated decades ago, and because high school grad workers are different from college grad workers in lots of important ways other than their degrees.

Think about the college wage premium as something like global temperature change, which tells us something very important about what is happening on earth but doesn't tell us much useful about what the weather will be like this week. We need other data to tell us whether to pack a jacket this week, and we need data other than the college wage premium to tell us whether a particular college degree makes sense financially for us.

By far the best outcomes for college graduates as compared to their high graduate peers come in finding a job. The unemployment rate for the average college graduate with a bachelor's degree has been about half the rate for the average worker with only a high school diploma in recent decades. Does that make a strong case for getting a college degree? Many observers and analysts, including former president Bill Clinton, make that argument repeatedly. How does the unemployment rate play out for recent graduates? In fact, the gap has gotten even bigger: The unemployment rate for high school grads under age twenty-four is 19 percent but under 5 percent for college grads, so there is indeed a big advantage here in being a college grad.

That is not true everywhere though. In several countries—South Korea, Switzerland, and as we saw earlier, China and Italy, to name a few—the unemployment rate is actually higher for college grads than for those with less than a high school education. In many countries, the rates are about equal. In fact, the gap between the unemployment rates for high school grads (and dropouts) compared to college grads in the United States is among the largest in the developed world.

The much lower unemployment rate among college grads in the United States is often taken as evidence that there are lots of jobs available that require college skills, but that conclusion does not follow. A college grad can do most any job that requires only a high school degree, and we know that college grads have been taking those high school jobs in record numbers. Doing so, in turn, leaves the high school grads without jobs. The big difference in the unemployment rates in the United States appears to be because the college grads take jobs that otherwise would have gone to high school grads.

We also know that the ability to earn that college wage premium requires getting a job that uses college-level skills. A college graduate in a job that requires only high school skills earns little more than a high school graduate in that job. After Richard Freeman found the surprising result that the wages of college graduates as compared to high school graduates fell sharply from 1969 to 1974, others started looking at what might happen when workers have more education than the jobs they hold requires. What they found, in studies outside the United States as well as here, is that wages are much lower when workers are overeducated for their jobs, very close to the level of those with education equal to the requirements, that job satisfaction is lower, that the individuals tend to remain underemployed and underpaid relative to their education, and so forth.

About one-third of U.S. workers are overeducated for their jobs, or put another way, underemployed, and they earn about half what their peers are paid for jobs that require the degree they have. Of course, those who are now in jobs where they are underemployed do not necessarily stay in those jobs forever, but the unpleasant finding is that the burdens of being underemployed initially tends to persist for a long time, in some studies for decades.[7] It makes a difference if someone graduates from college and waits tables for a few months before getting a good job, versus the graduate who remains a bartender for years because he or she can't find a job that requires a college degree. Life is short, though, and time spent underemployed is difficult. In a context where individuals are increasingly asked to pay for their own skills, asking them not to worry about the odds of being overskilled is unrealistic.

Not surprisingly, the experience of being overqualified is greater at the entry level, when one has fewer skills that are learned on the job. The likelihood of being overqualified varies by field and is less where the labor market is strong. Figure 3.1 shows the probability of a college grad being underemployed based on his or her college major. Note that the probability of being underemployed is only trivially different for business majors, perhaps the most vocationally oriented field, and liberal arts majors, sometimes thought to be the least vocationally oriented.

What happens to those college grads who find themselves in jobs that require only a high school degree? Fewer of them are getting the better jobs that don't require a college degree, defined here as those that pay $45,000 or more. Recent grads who are only a year or so out of college have not done nearly as well as have the average college grad, especially since 2007 and the Great Recession, when many were likely to have taken jobs that traditionally only high school grads did. The bottom 10 percent of recent college grads are earning less than the average wage for high school grads, but of course, that may always be true because some college grads choose career paths like theater or arts that, at least initially, pay very little. A different set of measures shows the range of experience that recent college grads have when they don't get

FIGURE 3.1. Employment Outcomes for Recent College Graduates by Major, 2009–2011

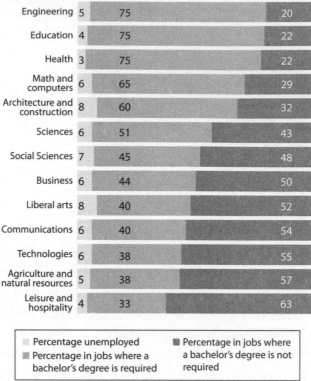

Major	Percentage unemployed	Percentage in jobs where a bachelor's degree is required	Percentage in jobs where a bachelor's degree is not required
Engineering	5	75	20
Education	4	75	22
Health	3	75	22
Math and computers	6	65	29
Architecture and construction	8	60	32
Sciences	6	51	43
Social Sciences	7	45	48
Business	6	44	50
Liberal arts	8	40	52
Communications	6	40	54
Technologies	6	38	55
Agriculture and natural resources	5	38	57
Leisure and hospitality	4	33	63

■ Percentage unemployed
■ Percentage in jobs where a bachelor's degree is required
■ Percentage in jobs where a bachelor's degree is not required

Notes: Recent college graduates are those aged twenty-two to twenty-seven with a bachelor's degree or higher. All figures exclude those currently enrolled in school. Because of rounding, figures in each bar may not sum to one hundred.
Source: Janelle Jones and John Schmitt, *A College Degree Is No Guarantee* (Washington, DC: Center for Economic and Policy Research, May 2014), http://www.cepr.net/documents/black-coll -grads-2014-05.pdf.

a job that requires their degree. Compared to the older, average grad, they are less likely to get a good job, more likely to get a poor job, and more likely to work part-time, and those differences have increased substantially since 2000.[8]

Whether employers are helped by having overskilled workers is a different question. One could imagine that they might be, if they redesigned the jobs to allow these people to do something different. Not all employers have that capability, of course, and studies investigating the question report no effect, with others finding negative effects and relatively few finding positive effects on employer performance from having overqualified workers.[9]

Being overqualified seems to be related to one of the more unpleasant findings about the experience of recent college graduates, who have graduated during an economic downturn, and that is that both diminished wages and prospects for better jobs persist for a decade or more. Some of that happens because of having to take a job with employers that are much less attractive than one would choose in better times, but much of it happens because movement out of those bad initial employers slows down. Because employers want to hire applicants with experience who already fit their profile, starting out in a poor job or with a poor employer makes it more difficult for the employee to find a better situation. For the most able graduates who get jobs, the negative effects last five years or so. For the least able, the effects are noticeable a decade or more after.[10]

It is certainly bad luck to graduate during or, worse, at the beginning of a downturn in the economy or even in the field you are trying to enter. It may be possible to duck that bad luck, though, something we consider shortly.

A Better Way to Measure the Payoff from College

The preceding caveats about relying on the college wage premium as the indicator of whether a college degree will pay off in the future are probably dwarfed by the fact that doing so ignores the cost of going to college, including obvious costs like tuition. Those costs can be big, really big. It is certainly possible that college grads will earn more than they would have if they had not gone to college and still not earn enough to pay off the costs of attending college.

When we ask whether something pays off, one answer is whether it covers its costs. Will we earn back the cost of going to college with those higher wages? Another answer to whether college pays off is whether what the graduate earns from it over time is at least as good as other investments that could have been made with the costs of going to college. The way to answer that question is with the financial measure of the rate of return on those investments.

Calculating the rate of return on a financial investment is a straightforward exercise. There is little debate over what the returns have been for an investment in a Fortune 100 company. But that is not the case for estimates of the returns on a college education. They are all over the map. Why is that? In part because the costs are not so easy to calculate, the returns are also hard to calculate, and especially because there is nothing particularly standard about college educations.

Let's start with the costs. While tuition, room and board, and other charges are pretty clear, possible amounts of financial aid are less so. Then how should we calculate the "cost" of the time involved in college? What should we assume students would be doing otherwise? If they were working, what would they be doing, and how much would they be earning?

And complicating the calculation are points most people ignore: What if the student takes more than four years to graduate? What if he or she does not graduate at all? One or both of these troubling outcomes happen to the majority of students who enter college every year.

Then how should we think about the returns? The graduates would have been earning something even if they didn't go to college, so not everything they earn should be credited to the college. Once again, because more privileged and able people tend to go to college, they likely would be earning more than a typical person without a college degree. Then we have the problem, as they say in finance, that past returns are not necessarily indicative of future returns. Should we assume that one's wages in the future will be the same as they are for the average employee at the moment? That may be our best guess, but it may not be especially accurate.

Finally we have the problem that different bachelor's degrees are not comparable from a labor-market perspective. A finance degree from an elite college positions one in a completely different labor market from a dance degree granted by a mediocre college. The variance in prospects across colleges and across degrees is so great that talking about "average" returns is irrelevant for an individual making a financial decision about which college to attend.

How one addresses these different issues, or whether they are addressed, explains why the estimates of the returns on a college degree vary so much. The Brookings Institution's Hamilton Project, for example, calculates that the rate of return will be 15 percent per year, a terrific rate that beats all standard financial investments.[11] These returns, though, assume that everyone who enters college will graduate and that they will do so in four years, a heroic assertion at best, and that there is nothing different between the average person who stops his or her education with high school and the person who goes on to college and completes college except for that degree. They also assume that the college wage premium for every age group will be the same over the lifetime of a new graduate as it is now—that is, when today's graduate turns thirty, the wage premium will be what it is for those who are age thirty now; when he or she turns fifty in twenty-five years or so, it will be what it is for those who are age fifty today. As a reminder, the college wage premium right now is the highest in modern times.

Suppose someone offered you an opportunity to invest in a stock and promised you a rate of 15 percent per year on the basis of the assumption that current performance, which is at its peak, will remain unchanged. Would you take it? It certainly sounds attractive, but the person making the offer would be arrested because security laws do not allow one to make claims like that for stocks precisely because there is no reason to believe it will be true—hence the caveat that prior returns are not necessarily proof of future returns. But claims like these are commonplace in the world of college education.

There are other estimates of the return on a college degree that don't turn out so well. One of the best known and most sophisticated is conducted by the PayScale company, whose main business is to collect salary data. It works backward from personal information from about 17 million individuals to estimate the return on specific college degrees, in fact, for specific colleges. It makes some crucial and more realistic assumptions, such as including the probability that a student will take longer than four years to graduate from a given college. But it makes a similar assumption that future wage premiums will look like current wage premiums, albeit using a college-by-college measure of the wage premium.

What PayScale reports is a college-by-college rate of return for bachelor's degrees from 1,310 different colleges, and those results are stunning in their variety. Brigham Young and Georgia Tech both top the list with a 12.5 percent annual return, but there are many schools that generate a negative return. The return at about one hundred colleges fails to keep up with inflation. Overall, the rate of return in this study is about half that given in the Brookings report.[12]

Businessweek teamed up with PayScale to do a separate calculation that included some additional and, it turns out, crucial adjustments, such as accounting for the fact that the college grads would have earned more if they had not gone to college than would the average high school grad. The reason, as we've noted throughout, is that they tend to have more abilities and relevant resources even before going to college. Out of the 835 colleges *Businessweek* examined, a stunning 191—almost one in four—had a negative return on investment.[13] The best thing a student in those schools could do to improve their rate of return is to leave. How much of that poor performance is due to the attributes of students who attend—just as how much of the success of graduates of elite schools is due to what the students arrive on campus with—is hard to know.

There are lots of things one could quibble with in these studies. They exclude from the college sample individuals who go on to earn graduate degrees, which may take out some of the most able of the people who graduate from college, but they also ignore loans and their interest costs of attending college, which are now a huge part of the costs of college.

The big problem in any estimate of the future returns on education, though, is the need to guess where wages for college grads will be in the future. We know that the college wage premium has been all over the map in previous generations, and while one could tell a story saying that its current peak level will remain there for decades, there are equally compelling stories saying that it will not. For example, fans of the idea that technology is destiny argue that modern computing power is rapidly eliminating the jobs that don't require much thinking at the same time that it is creating lots of new opportunities for the educated. Other fans of technology is destiny say that hands-on skills, such as skilled trades, which don't require traditional classroom educations, are about the only jobs that computers can't do, so they are about the only ones that will remain in demand. College is a waste in that view.

So where does that leave an individual trying to decide what to do about college? The first conclusion, which is a big one, is that statements about what college will do on average for a student are irrelevant because the variation in results across schools and across fields is so great. It would be like using the average temperate of the earth—fifty-five degrees—to decide whether to wear a coat today. It is a school-by-school story, perhaps even a major-by-major one within each school. There are colleges where attending them will do nothing for your future earnings, and while that may not be the only factor in deciding where to go to college, it ought to be something you know.

The second conclusion is the reminder that we just don't know with much certainty what things will look like in the future, and the farther out the guess, the less valid and useful guesses will be. The baby boomers among us will remember when the standard advice for career success was to get a job with a big company because it would take care of you because that's the way things had operated before. How well did that work out?

The wrong conclusion to draw from all this uncertainty is to just give up: We don't know what will happen, so there is no point trying to figure it out. We can do better than that.

One of the things we do know is that current evidence beats forecasts especially when it comes to something as complicated as the labor market. Some of the most useful information about college outcomes is from a group called CollegeMeasures.org, which provides evidence on first-year earnings for college graduates by college and also by major within different states. There are clear limits as to what

FIGURE 3.2. Higher Education Pays, but a Lot More for Some Graduates than for Others

a) First-Year Earnings of Graduates with Associate's Versus Bachelor's Degrees, by State

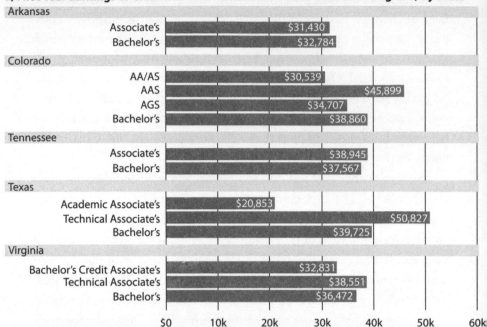

b) First-Year Earnings of Completers with Subbaccalaureate Credentials, by State

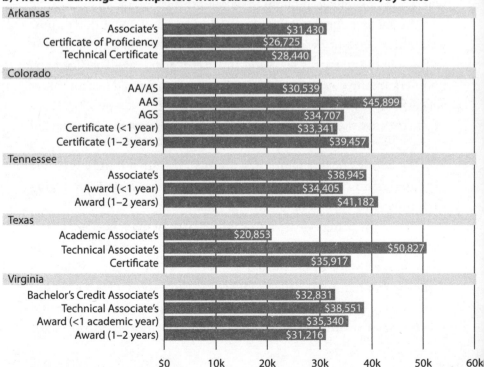

Source: "College Education Pays: But a Lot More for Some Students than Others," September 3, 2013, CollegeMeasures.org/category/reports.aspx.

information like this can tell us about the future, but at least it's not a guess. What we learn from them is more "it depends," but we get a sense of what success depends on.

One thing we learn is that major can trump degree. Two-year community college degrees can pay more than average four-year degrees when the former are in a technical field that is in demand, in some cases stunningly so. In Texas, for example, recent grads with associate degrees in nuclear power technology earn just under $100,000, while those in fire prevention and fire services earn close to $90,000. Other two-year degrees, even if they are in technical areas, pay very little. Texas grads with a two-year degree in animal sciences are paid less than $10,000 per year, which implies that on average even those who are working can't get full-time jobs. It doesn't seem to be the case that degrees in animal sciences are less challenging than degrees in fire prevention are, so it is not that the pay difference is due to sorting out more able students.

In the same field, though, the difference between a two-year and a four-year degree matters a lot. In information technology, for example, a bachelor's degree in Texas pays about double—$60,000—the average salary of two-year associate degree graduates. Not all technical degrees pay off, bursting another common assertion, and that is most noticeably so for STEM degrees. Again in Texas, a two-year sociology degree pays off a lot better than the equivalent chemistry, biology, or math degree, which is stunning given all the talk about the alleged demand in STEM fields. At the bachelor's level, that changes, as math degrees in particular start to pay off more, but the sociology degree still pays better than the biology degree.

Going to the Better College: Does It Pay?

For many high school students and their families, the goal is not just to get into college but to get into the best college they can. In some circles, you could think that a student's future is secured as soon as he or she is accepted by an elite institution. These students will then become part of a social network of rich and famous peers who will guide them along, employers will compete for their services, the key to the executive washroom will always be theirs, and life will be good.

It is easy to see how that picture developed. So many of the most prominent public figures have elite educations that it is easy to see that people with degrees from more selective colleges do better. Harvard and especially Yale have educated every U.S. president since Ronald Reagan left office and every current Supreme Court justice. My studies with Monika Hamori and Rocio Bonet of corporate careers show that a remarkable 14 percent of all top executives in the biggest corporations in 1980 graduated from one of the eight Ivy League schools. While that figure has slid a bit with time, it was still 10 percent as of 2011, as graduates of elite schools shifted to better-paying fields such as hedge funds.[14]

The elite schools have been elite for so long that the notion that they confer privilege to their alumni has been around for generations. Caroline Hoxby looked at the lifetime earnings of men who graduated from college from 1960 through 1982 and found that the alumni of the most selective schools earned roughly twice as much over their lifetime as those from less selective schools.[15]

Researchers at CollegeMeasures.org looked at the earnings of graduates from selective colleges in five states, with the caveat that they were then employed in that same state. They found that there was a considerable difference between the earnings of graduates from the most selective colleges as compared to those from the least selective. But for graduates of schools in the middle, the differences were modest at best.[16]

Determining why graduates in the same field from one set of colleges earn more than others takes us back to the screening question and the *Trading Places* story from Chapter 1. Is education valuable because what we learn in school is useful in the workplace, or is it valuable because schools select students who already have attributes that are useful in the workplace? As in the *Trading Places* story, could you get by with no education and a fake degree if you had street smarts? Fortunately for the elite colleges, their graduates seem to credit the colleges for much of their success. But researchers are not sure.

There are a number of very important differences across colleges, and we considered them in more detail in Chapter 2. However, a little secret of faculty who talk to their peers at other colleges—as everyone does—is that the basic courses in a given subject are almost identical across colleges. That is true for the intermediate courses in most subjects as well. The more standard the major, the more likely that is to be true. There can be big differences in the most advanced courses mainly on the basis of the distinction between being an undergraduate at a university where graduate students are also being taught as opposed to a college where that is not the case. But that difference is mainly important for those who are going on to graduate school. For students who finish college with a bachelor's degree, the content of the course work does not differ all that much across colleges. If we think that the classroom experiences alone are driving the results, it might be surprising to see income differences be as big as they are.

Can we tell the two explanations apart? The economists Stacey Dale and Alan Krueger had the novel idea of looking at students who were admitted to very selective colleges but then attended other, less selective colleges. What those students brought to the college party was pretty similar to those who were accepted by the elite colleges and attended those colleges. So if we compare what happens to those two groups of students after they graduate, we get a much better idea than ever before of what each type of college adds to the success of its graduates. Dale and Krueger found that students who were admitted to but did not attend very selective colleges earned roughly the same amount as those who actually attended those colleges. In other words, the better outcomes from those elite schools seemed to be driven by the fact that the students they accepted were more able when they arrived. The authors repeated the study with other data and found the same result.[17]

Those results may look like a knock-out blow to elite colleges, at least about the financial returns on college, but the authors did find some evidence in favor of a payoff from these colleges. One was that lower-income and minority students who were admitted to elite schools did earn more, other things being equal, if they graduated from that elite school than if they went elsewhere. Perhaps those elite schools can provide some substitute for the advantages that better-off students otherwise have. The other finding was that there was also an earnings premium associated with attending a more expensive school, independent of the selectivity of the school. Schools with higher tuition apparently were using the money to do something that benefited their students.

Of course, there are always other studies. One examined the earnings of students who were admitted to the unnamed but most selective of the state schools in Texas as compared to those who were rejected and attended other schools in Texas. The advantage of examining this context is that the criteria for admissions to the University of Texas were reasonably straightforward, so it was possible to compare students who were just over the bar for admissions and attended UT Austin (I guess we just gave away the elite school) with those who just missed making it in and went elsewhere. The idea here is that the two groups of students were pretty equal except for the college they attended. The students who just made it in and graduated from UT Austin earned about 20 percent more than those who just missed getting in. Twenty percent is a sizeable difference, but it is far short of what we would see as the average gap between graduating from an elite versus a nonelite school.[18]

Okay, so it does pay off at least somewhat to go to an elite school. A study from Israel suggests how it works. The researchers compared the earnings over time of graduates from the most elite, established university to those from a newer, less prestigious college. Initially, even the best graduates of the new college earned less than those from the elite university. But over time, as the newer college became better known and the reputation of its graduates grew, the wages of its graduates also increased. Now students with similar abilities from the two schools have similar earnings. It took a while for employers to experience the graduates of the newer college and figure out that they were just as good. After that, the wages went up for all its graduates. This suggests that employers are using the college brand as a proxy for the ability of its graduates and that better information about the graduates changes the "price" paid for them.[19]

Using the brand or reputation of the college as a proxy for the quality of its graduates has the basic problem that few graduates are average: There are stinkers graduating from elite schools and stars graduating from unremarkable colleges. If you use that brand value to hire, you'll be overpaying some people and missing out on some really good ones who would be cheaper. Rather than relying on the reputation of the college, why not just test the graduates yourself? You could ignore the brand of the college and the big wage premium that comes with it. There is some evidence from the United Kingdom that this works. The premium paid for college grads is less where employers do testing like this, apparently because they could find good hires at colleges where the graduates are cheaper.[20]

So you'd think every employer would do that kind of searching and testing, but they don't. Lots of them decide to recruit from only a select set of colleges without looking at graduates from others. They decide where to hire on the basis of all kinds of reasons, but where the bosses went to college is the one you hear surprisingly often.

One company that takes sorting out the value of different colleges seriously is India-based Tata. It has turned this analytic approach into an art form by assessing all its new college hires on the basis of the school where they graduated, considering their job performance, how long they stay with Tata, and also how much the company had to pay to hire them. As a result, the company targets its recruiting at schools that provide the biggest bang for the buck. Some of the elite U.S. business schools didn't make the cut, even though their graduates were great employees, because those graduates didn't stay very long and were quite expensive to hire.

A problem with looking at the average results for graduates of a particular college is that average doesn't mean typical. One Bill Gates in the graduating class could make the average salary skyrocket for the entire alumni base of a college. A possibly apocryphal story from the University of North Carolina found that its highest paid major in the period studied was sociology, largely because of one graduate with that major, the basketball superstar Michael Jordan.

Another Texas study looked to see whether the average effects we see from graduating from an elite college apply across the board for all students graduating from the same college. These researchers looked to see how the top earners from elite schools fared relative to the top earners from average schools, again in Texas. For UT Austin, the most selective of the state universities, the top earners did much better than did the top earners from the average schools, earning over 30 percent more. Perhaps the most surprising findings are that graduates of community colleges, the least selective schools, earned not much less than the grads from the average four-year schools when students of similar abilities were compared. And the highest earners among community college graduates actually earned more than the highest earners from the average four-year colleges.[21] College reputation may not be all it's cracked up to be when we are thinking about future earnings.

Several organizations now produce calculators that let you compare costs and outcomes across colleges:

- Calculating the Value from Different Colleges
- *The Chronicle of Higher Education's* College Reality Check (Collegerealitycheck.com)—includes limited wage data
- CollegeMeasures.org
- PayScale.com—wage outcomes and return on investment from college
- The White House's College Affordability and Transparency Center College Scorecard, http://www.whitehouse.gov/issues/education /higher-education/collegescore-card

Why are all these studies done in Texas? Well, it's a big place, and it has a lot of students. But there is also a story behind these studies that suggests some of the arcane challenges we have to overcome to examine the effects of college. A lot of people move around in the United States, especially when going to and leaving colleges. So it would be important to be able to follow them across states. The problem is that the federal government is prohibited from tracking students who move across states and analyzing the data about their education, by laws like the Family Educational Rights and Privacy Act. So only individual states can look at the relationship between students' performance and their outcomes in the job market, and they can only do it for those students who remain within their state after college. Some states are trying to share data with each other; but this is a big country, and it would be hard to get good information unless many states agreed to do so.

One place where elite colleges really do matter is when applying to graduate schools. Unlike employers, graduate programs really do care about the academic reputation of an undergraduate college, because they want to know how well students are prepared to do more academic work. Elite graduate schools tend to pick applicants from elite undergraduate programs. So if you want to be a lawyer, doctor, MBA, or especially a professor, it is much easier to be accepted into a graduate program, especially an elite one, if you graduated from one of the famous undergraduate programs.

Who Are the Winners?

All of these caveats can be applied when we look at the evidence as to which colleges have the best net payoff on the costs of going there. The PayScale ranking shows that the top schools are all ones turning out engineering and tech grads (see Table 3.1). Engineering is far from being the best paying field in the economy, so why would these schools be at the top? It isn't so much that their tech grads make more than those at other schools; it is that they don't have any programs in social work or English majors associated with low-wage fields that would pull the average down.

Wages for graduates of the Colorado School of Mines are hot now because extraction industries are hot. But the reason the return on investment of it (and also of the New York Maritime College) is so high is that they are both state universities where the costs are low. At the Maritime College, that's true even for out-of-state tuition. NYU's Polytechnic Institute (school of engineering) makes the list because

TABLE 3.1

RANK	SCHOOL NAME	TYPE	CATEGORY
1	Harvey Mudd College	Private not-for-profit	Private Schools, Liberal Arts, Engineering
2	California Institute of Technology (Caltech)	Private not-for-profit	Private Schools, Research Universities, Engineering
3	Polytechnic Institute of New York University (NYU-Poly)	Private not-for-profit	Private Schools, Research Universities, Engineering
4	Massachusetts Institute of Technology (MIT)	Private not-for-profit	Private Schools, Research Universities, Engineering
5	SUNY - Maritime College	Public (In-State)	State Schools, Engineering
6	Colorado School of Mines	Public (In-State)	State Schools, Engineering, Research Universities
7	SUNY - Maritime College	Public (Out-of-State)	State Schools, Engineering
8	Colorado School of Mines	Public (Out-of-State)	State Schools, Engineering, Research Universities
9	Stevens Institute of Technology	Private not-for-profit	Private Schools, Research Universities, Engineering

Source: College Salary Report, http://www.payscale.com/college-salary-report/bachelors.

of the very large percentage of students receiving financial aid. The large amount of aid per student helps the return for MIT students. Stevens Institute of Technology, despite being nowhere near as selective as the other engineering schools on the list, is also in their league in terms of the rate of return because so many students get financial aid. Cal Tech and Harvey Mudd, the leaders, are both very small, selective colleges whose alumni, disproportionately in engineering and very competent even before they got to college, just seem to make a lot of money. High completion rates here also help.

One of the caveats to studies about the wage returns from attending elite colleges has to do with preferences for locations—where one wants to work. Many employers look for new hires disproportionately from local colleges. It's easier to do interviews and other recruiting activities lo-

2012 COST	30 YEAR NET ROI	ANNUAL ROI	% AID	AVG AID AMOUNT	30 YEAR ROI WITH AID	ANNUAL ROI WITH AID
$221,700	$2,113,000	8.3%	69	$25,117	$2,217,000	10.6%
$213,000	$1,991,000	8.2%	58	$27,007	$2,103,000	11.0%
$214,300	$1,622,000	7.6%	97	$23,534	$1,728,000	10.1%
$215,700	$1,606,000	7.5%	65	$32,550	$1,739,000	11.0%
$90,530	$1,586,000	10.4%	43	$5,567	$1,611,000	11.6%
$107,100	$1,574,000	9.7%	66	$7,282	$1,607,000	11.1%
$124,800	$1,552,000	9.2%	43	$5,567	$1,552,000	9.2%
$170,900	$1,510,000	8.0%	66	$7,282	$1,510,000	8.0%
$237,300	$1,461,000	6.9%	95	$25,125	$1,574,000	9.2%

cally, ties with the schools are tighter given that executives running those companies are more likely to be graduates from the local schools, and internships are easier to arrange with local colleges because the students and the jobs are in the same place. If you want a job in San Francisco, it might actually be better to go to the University of San Francisco than to attend a more elite college far away, such as the University of Michigan, because you will have better access to local employers.

On the other hand, if you want a job with big companies that have national or international footprints or with a federal government agency, such as the State Department, it is better to go to a college with a national reputation like the University of Michigan.

Schools that do not have those national reputations and that don't have many local employers nearby, especially rural colleges, have the job-hunting deck stacked against their graduates. Students at colleges that have those elite reputations and that also have lots of good employers nearby—think Stanford, the University of Chicago, Columbia University—are doubly blessed in the hunt for jobs.

4

The Cost of
Going to College

GIVEN HOW MANY colleges there are in the United States and how many are just hankering to have your student attend there, the biggest challenge for most all families about going to college isn't getting in; it's paying for it. The United States spends more money in total and per capita on education than any other country, but the reason for that is because we spend so much on college.

For students, more important than the fact that we spend a lot on college in the United States is that we expect the students and their families to pay for it. Students and their families here pay a whopping six times more for college than the average for their peers across Western countries in Europe and Japan.[1] (We examine the option of attending foreign colleges later.)

Even those people who don't care about the economic return from college or those who are expecting a big payoff from attending college still have to pay for it up front. That is why cost is such a big deal for virtually everyone thinking about going to college.

The cost of college is also the easiest part of the equation to understand about whether college pays off. Other things being equal, the less you pay for something, the greater the net benefits from it are likely to be. Knowing whether those other things are equal across colleges is the tricky part.

Tuition costs at elite private schools grab the headlines, but only about 8 percent of college students attend schools where tuition and fees exceed $40,000 per year. That would be a bargain price at the most selective private schools, where the costs are at least 25 percent higher. Room-and-board charges for students attending school away from home do not vary all that much; but the tuition charges are quite different depending on the school, so that is what drives the cost differences. As Figure 4.1 indicates, the cost of attending college has over time become an increasingly important factor in determining which schools students pick.

The annual survey of college freshmen conducted by UCLA shows us that students still see academic reputation as the prime criterion for picking colleges, but costs and financial aid have become increasingly important, just about catching up to the concern about whether that the college can get them a good job. Perhaps influenced

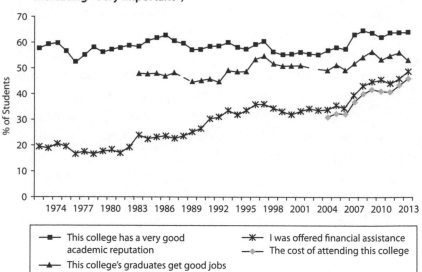

FIGURE 4.1. Top Reasons for Choosing Current Institution (Percentage Indicating "Very Important")

Source: Higher Education Research Institute at UCLA, "The American Freshman: National Norms, Fall 2013" (Research Brief, March 2014), http://www.heri.ucla.edu /briefs/TheAmericanFreshman2013-Brief.pdf

by their parents, students applying to colleges really are trying to figure out where college will pay off.

What complicates our understanding of the costs of attending college is financial aid, which may also be the most important arrangement in the United States for creating opportunity for advancement in society. Financial aid is a bit of a mystery to most participants in higher education, and in part it is made so on purpose to keep people from trying to "game" the system.

Financial aid is hard to understand because it is individualized to the circumstances of each applicant, so knowing what one family got doesn't tell you much about what you will get. It's also more mysterious now because financial aid is no longer just about helping poor kids get through college. That is, it is no longer just based on a family's financial circumstances. "Merit-based aid" is also a source of competitive advantage to help schools secure the best students and, in the process, compete with each other. Unfortunately, merit aid has also made it more challenging to determine what the costs at a particular college will be, not unlike trying to buy a car.

Financial aid can be quite complicated in the sense that it involves lots of formulas and data. That doesn't mean one needs to be a deep expert on it to avoid making mistakes, however. A reasonably simple understanding of the basic principles goes a very long way, perhaps almost all the way, to getting as much as possible out of it. But before getting into the discounting that comes from financial aid, it is important to start out with a look at posted tuitions and fees for attending college and the great variation among them.

Sticker Shock

The experience of shopping for a new car usually begins with sticker shock when one first looks at the retail price posted on the window of each new car. Very few people end up paying that price, of course, but seeing it for the first time is a kick in the teeth to most people hunting for a new car for the first time.

With college costs, that kick in the teeth for parents comes with seeing the figures about the estimated costs per year to send their children to college. It is especially brutal because most people are not routinely in the market for college educations as they might be for cars. They remember their own college experiences and tuition costs, twenty years or more earlier, and they are not prepared for how much those costs have climbed since then.

Although inflation raises all prices a lot over time, that's not the main story in higher education. As Figure 4.2 suggests, the real cost of tuition and fees, discounting for inflation, have gone up enormously over the past thirty years, outpacing the increases in virtually all other prices. Private colleges, where the price has increased by

FIGURE 4.2. Inflation-Adjusted Published Tuition and Fees Relative to 1983–1984, 1983–1984 to 2013–2014 (1983–1984 = 100)

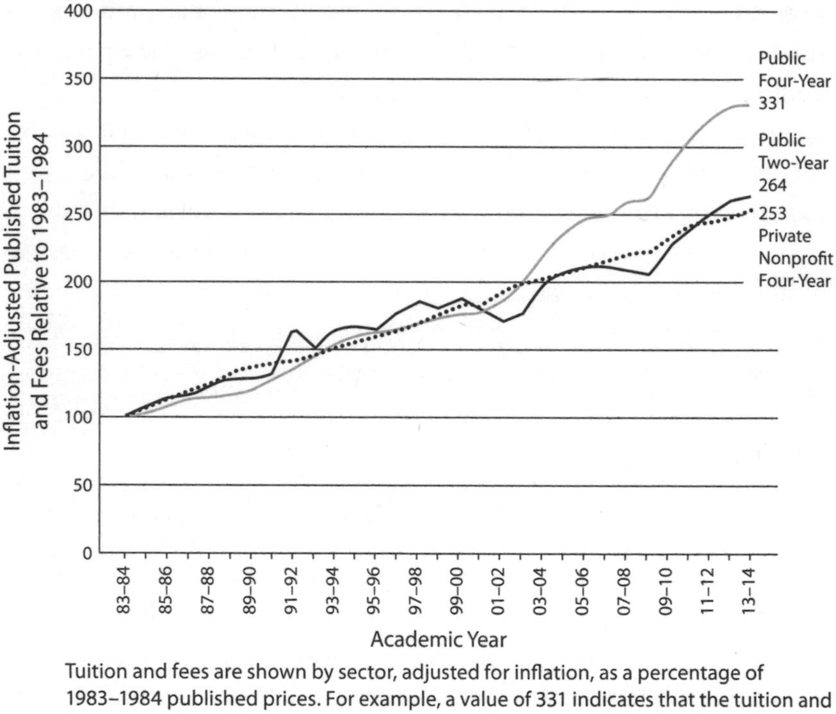

Tuition and fees are shown by sector, adjusted for inflation, as a percentage of 1983–1984 published prices. For example, a value of 331 indicates that the tuition and fee price in the public four-year sector in 2013–2014 is 3.31 times as high as it was in 1983–1984, after adjusting for increases in the Consumer Price Index.
Source: The College Board, Annual Survey of Colleges (Princeton, NJ: 2014).

250 percent, are actually a model of restraint compared to state colleges, where the increase has been 330 percent. To put these costs in some perspective, remember that the line showing changes in real wages over this same period would be a straight horizontal line at the 100 percent mark, barely rising over the past thirty years.

And why the separate charges for fees, in addition to tuition? In part it is an internal accounting issue to separate the charges associated with standard academic content (tuition) from charges for other things that are a different part of the college experience, such as extracurricular activities (fees). Those other experiences have grown considerably. In part, separate charges keeps the tuition charges smaller than if fees were rolled into them, like charging separately for floor mats when buying a car.

Why have the increases been so big at state universities? Those in the middle of the United States have had the smallest increases, although note that these increases represent the amount above inflation, so a 26 percent rise in real costs at state four-year colleges in the middle of the United States over the past ten years is not trivial. It is the costs at public colleges in the South and West that have truly exploded, up by 65 and 86 percent, respectively, in real terms (see Table 4.1).

The reason that costs have gone up so much as well as the explanation as to where they have gone up has to do with politics, specifically

TABLE 4.1. Ten-Year Dollar Change and Percentage Change in Inflation-Adjusted Tuition and Fees, by Sector and College Board Region, 2003–2004 to 2013–2014

Region	Public Two-Year Ten-Year $ Change	Public Two-Year Ten-Year % Change	Public Four-Year Ten-Year $ Change	Public Four-Year Ten-Year % Change	Private Nonprofit Four-Year Ten-Year $ Change	Private Nonprofit Four-Year Ten-Year % Change
Middle States	521	13	1,955	26	5,967	23
Midwest	790	27	2,685	39	6,279	28
New England	934	25	3,322	42	7,271	24
South	1,063	46	3,144	65	5,847	28
Southwest	622	36	2,940	59	9,022	48
West	968	70	4,048	86	3,240	14

Source: College Board, *Trends in College Pricing* (Princeton, NJ: 2014).

the willingness of taxpayers and their representatives to support college education. California is driving the average results for western states, although the others have had a somewhat similar experience. The state college and especially the state university system in California was famously good and cheap in the 1960s, but by the 1980s, taxpayer revolts began to squeeze tax payments and the revenue available to support higher education even as enrollments exploded. That squeeze has continued. When state colleges and universities cannot get additional revenue from the government, or in the case of California and states in the South, where budgets have actually been cut, the solution has been to raise tuition. When tuition starts out low, as it had been in many of these states, the percentage increases are huge.

The roller-coaster pattern of support, followed by the steep decline since the Great Recession, is countered by the reasonably steady increase in student enrollments. The gap between appropriations per full-time-equivalent student and the number of enrollees is the big problem facing public education in the United States.

Here again, though, the variation across states is huge. The Appendix contains data state-by-state on tuition and state financial support. Alaska contributes the most to covering the costs of college in its state universities, over $17,000 per enrollee. New Hampshire contributes the least, less than $2,400. That helps explain why New Hampshire has the highest tuition charges of any state university system, while Alaska has the second lowest. But state aid doesn't completely explain differences in tuition across state universities. The cheapest is a western school—Wyoming—at about $4,000 per year, versus Penn State, the most expensive at roughly $18,000 per year.

Why not just go to the schools in the states that have the cheapest tuition? State governments saw that one coming long ago. Cheaper tuition at their state universities is a huge perk for constituents, and they don't want anyone who could not vote for them getting that benefit. Why should someone whose family did not pay taxes in that state get the benefit of taxpayer-supported education? So states sock it to out-of-state students who want to go to their universities, charging them as much as $20,000 more than they charge state residents. The University of Michigan at Ann Arbor has the highest out-of-state tuition at $40,000, but other flagship universities like Berkeley and UCLA are not far behind.

Out-of-state tuition is typically double or triple the price of tuition for state residents, which often brings it close to the price of private schools. Financial aid for students at state universities is more limited than for those at private schools, and it may be even more limited for out-of-state students at public universities than for in-state students. So cost is a big hurdle for any students thinking about attending state universities in other states.

If you are a student from Minnesota with a hankering to attend the University of California at San Diego, what might you do to handle the costs? There are businesses that have come to the rescue. Firms like In-State Angels (https://www.instateangels.com/learn/faq/) walk out-of-state students through the often complicated process of becoming a resident in the state where their preferred state university sits. It can save such students and their parents a ton of money, of course, at the expense of that state's taxpayers.

There are some differences across colleges in other aspects of college costs, such as room and board. Private schools again cost more but not by much, and generally that pays for swishier dormitories. The main factor in understanding the considerable variation in the costs of going to college remains differences in tuition charges. To see what the sticker prices are for any college in the United States, go to the Department of Education's College Navigator website: http://nces.ed.gov/collegenavigator/.

People are fascinated with the differences in tuition and fees across colleges, but that is really focusing on the sticker price. As with car buying, what people actually pay to go to college is usually quite different from the sticker price. The reason, of course, as noted earlier, is financial aid, the process of cutting the price for different students on the basis of their ability to pay and, more recently, on the basis of how much the school wants them.

The Practice of Financial Aid

The big puzzle about college costs is that students pay different amounts for the same college experience, and they also pay for it in different ways. As with airline tickets, you might find someone in the seat next to you in class who paid half what you did to get in because of financial aid. Think of it as a rich uncle—mainly Uncle Sam—who has decided to make it easier for some kids, mainly poor ones, to go to college. Think of it also as policy decisions made by the government and also by the individual colleges that are designed to offset other decisions that have made college more expensive over time.

A lot of people without much money go to college every year, including 19 percent of students whose families are poor enough to receive food stamps or similar support. Financial aid is what enables them to overcome their limited financial resources. Eighty percent of students in college apply for it, and virtually all get something. In fact, it's a safe bet that many students who don't apply would have gotten some assistance if they had applied.

We can think of financial aid as the practice of lowering the price of attending college, sometimes dramatically so, for different students. The traditional goal was to make college affordable for those who would otherwise have no chance of being able to pay for it. Cynics might also describe financial aid as price discrimination, charging different prices to different students on the basis of their ability to pay, much as airlines charge more to people who really have to travel at the last minute as compared to those who can plan well in advance. That analogy is not really accurate in most schools, however, because the government rather than the school is providing the aid. It's more about changing who sits on the plane than it is about filling it up. A better analogy is probably health care, where the government pays the treatment costs of those patients without the means to pay themselves.

Whether you are a cynic on this issue also depends on what you think the "true" price of college is. If you think students from rich families pay more than the real cost of their education, then you are in the price discrimination camp. If you think those students pay something like the true cost and poor students pay less, then you are likely to see financial aid as perhaps the most important, meritocratic arrangement in contemporary society for helping kids from lower-income families to get ahead.

Tuition clearly does not cover the total costs of education at most colleges, and the evidence for that comes from the fact that government subsidies, especially in public institutions, and gifts and endowments, especially in private institutions, contribute substantially to the costs of those operations. Whether the sticker price that students without financial aid pay covers the costs for each student is a different question that is very hard to answer. There is a sense that at some high-priced private schools, such students overpay to create some of the aid that goes to poorer students in the form of financial aid. But the fact that for-profit colleges have stayed out of the traditional campus-based undergraduate market tells us that it is not a moneymaker.

While there have always been some other forms of support—athletic scholarships in particular—need-based aid to help poor students go to college was for decades the only game in town. Government aid to students goes back to the GI Bill, which paid much of the college costs for service men and women after World War II. What we now think as more traditional financial aid begins in the United States in the 1950s at private colleges where resources were made available to support students who otherwise could not afford to attend college.

Before then, if a student did not have the money to go to college, there was only one real option, and that was to work one's way through college with jobs on campus or nearby and then in the summer as well. Assuming one could find a job, it was possible to do that because college was relatively cheap. In the 1920s, for example, tuition and fees at the Wharton School were $270 for the year. Twenty years later in 1940, it had only risen to $420 per year, and in 1950 it was $625.[2] In 1950, the minimum wage was $0.75 per hour, which meant that working in even the lowest paid job could cover college costs in roughly twenty weeks of full-time work. (Of course, that assumes living at home and not having to pay anything else, such as taxes!) This was not easy, of course, but possible. Today it would take 164 weeks of full-time work at the minimum wage to pay current tuition and fee costs at elite colleges. Some of that is because the minimum wage, discounting for inflation, is a lot lower than it was in the 1950s, but most of it has to do with the higher costs of college.

Financial aid the way we know it today started in 1954 when ninety-five northeastern colleges got together to form the College Scholarship Service (CSS). The CSS established the criteria to measure college students and their families' ability to contribute to their education, criteria based on family income. By 1956, most private schools that offered aid to students were using that standard model, and it is something many parents would recognize today. Applicants paid a fee to the CSS, which then determined the ability of the applicant and his or her family to pay and suggested to the individual college the amount of aid necessary to allow that student to enroll. The principle that financial aid should be based on need—family income— and that the determinations should be common across schools was well in place.

Public policy entered financial aid for traditional students with the 1958 National Defense Education Act, which pioneered loans, backed by the government, to support low-income students. From there, we were off to the races with one new aid package after another from the federal government as we tried to beat the Soviet Union in the race for scientific and technological supremacy.[3]

The effect of public policy in this period, and arguably the intent as well, was to increase access to college. States expanded their college systems enormously, especially in New York and California, and kept tuition low. Financial aid was the arrangement for increasing access at private colleges. The goal was also to do so in a manner that was consistent across applicants and colleges. Students with similar needs got similar financial aid from their state and especially the federal government.

The practices of colleges with their own, private aid did much the same thing. They believed that giving access to college to more low-income students was a very important goal and that the best way to do that was to target the available aid to those with the greatest need. The criterion for federal grants was standard across all colleges, targeted to the costs of attending public colleges and universities. Private schools and more expensive public institutions used loans to make up the difference between the costs of attending their schools and grants.

The phrase "need-blind admission policy" became common in this period, and it meant that admission decisions were made without considering the financial aid implications associated with each applicant. So concerned were leading colleges that they might inadvertently use financial aid to compete for students, and in the process reduce resources that could have been used to help more students, that they created the Overlap Group among the wealthiest schools—the Ivy League, MIT, and others—where they compared who they had admitted to ensure that a student accepted to more than one school in the group received identical financial aid packages from each school. The U.S. Justice Department ruled that the practice of the Overlap Group violated antitrust law, essentially affirming that college was a business governed more like a market than most financial aid administrators thought, and a consent decree in 1993 put the Overlap Group out of business.[4]

In the generation from the 1960s through the early 1990s, it was virtually impossible to get financial aid just because you were smart. A review of aid options in 1990 found that the merit awards that did exist were virtually all honorific, good for one's ego but not much more.[5]

Today, things have changed, but the big money for financial aid is still need based, and most of it still comes from the federal government. That aid takes three forms:

- *Grants.* This is aid that does not have to be repaid. (A scholarship is a grant as well, typically one based on merit.) The biggest grant program is the federal government's Pell Grants. Every student who gets need-based financial aid gets a Pell

Grant, and the average Pell Grant in 2012–2013 was $3,650. States also have grant programs, and the average state grant was $670 in 2012. All of the state grants in Georgia are now merit based, and other states like Florida and South Carolina have also shifted their support from need to merit aid. Whether other colleges will move in that direction remains an open question.

- *Work-study.* This is a program that provides aid to schools to employ eligible students in part-time jobs. Most of the aid comes from the federal government, but some states provide funds for it as well. About 6 percent of college students have work-study positions, about one-third report that their job was in some way related to their courses (they weren't just working in the cafeteria), and they earn an average of $2,850 per year.

- *Loans.* These are repayable after graduation. Most student loans are backed in some way by the federal government, but there are also state loans and unsubsidized loans from the colleges themselves. Loans have become increasingly important, and I talk more about them later.

Along with tuition, financial aid has also gone up considerably in recent years, doubling from 2002–2003 to 2012–2013. The biggest increase is in loans, which are far less attractive to students in that they only delay payment. Unsubsidized loans, the most expensive and least attractive, are up 156 percent over that same period. Although the total number of students has also increased over the decade, the value of financial aid has increased per student in constant dollars from $11,000 in 2002–2003 to $15,000 in 2012–2013, a substantial jump, although nowhere near as much as tuition has increased.[6] The federal government provides an unusually user-friendly website that describes most everything about the different types of financial aid, who is eligible for what, and how each type works, at https://studentaid.ed.gov/.

> **How About Just Make It Up? Faking the College Degree**
>
> It's certainly cheaper just to lie about having a college degree, and a third of hiring managers report seeing false information about academic degrees and qualifications on job applications. That includes some prominent executives, such as Veritas Software Corp's CFO, who it turns out did not have a Stanford MBA; Bausch & Lomb's CEO, who didn't have an NYU MBA; Yahoo's CEO, who did not have a computer science degree; and Radio Shack's CEO, who didn't have a degree at all. Finding out whether someone actually has a degree from a particular school is harder than you'd think because of privacy rules: The person in question has to give the school permission to say. But now there are software companies making it easier to prove that you really have that degree to any possible employer, and the pressure to do so may make it more difficult to cheat. (These examples come from Vivian Giang and Jhaneel Lockhart, "Busted: This Is What Happened to 10 Executives Who Lied About Their Resumes," *Business Insider*, May 7, 2012. The information on tracking software and on the hiring managers survey is from Melissa Korn, "Soon, You'll Have to Tell the Truth on Your Resume," *Wall Street Journal*, September 20, 2014.)

Critics of higher education say that financial aid and especially increases in financial aid over time have really just been a means for allowing colleges to raise their prices. After all, what is the constraint to paying more if the students and their families aren't paying for it? Of course, that argument would only apply to government-provided aid (colleges that give aid out of their own budgets to try to get it back through higher prices would be wasting their time). That argument assumes that colleges are like businesses operating with the goal of making money. If they were, though, the elite colleges could double their tuition and still fill up the classes. There are more than enough wealthy families willing to pay to get their children into the best colleges. Many of those families already pay far more than the cost of college for private college-prep elementary and secondary schools designed to give those students a leg up in the admissions process. Nor would colleges bother giving need-based aid. They'd just keep the money and admit richer kids.

It is true that without financial aid, far fewer students could afford to go to college, and many colleges would be forced either to close their doors or to find some very inexpensive way to deliver something like a college experience. The incentive to cut costs and tuition is already there, of course, because costs matter to parents and students now. That is why merit aid works and why public colleges are attractive. The biggest change if we got rid of financial aid would be to keep poor kids out of college.

The most important story in financial aid in the past generation may be the rise of merit-based aid, based on attributes of students other than their financial need. The largest merit-based aid program is the Georgia Hope Scholarships, providing college grants to Georgia high school students on the basis of their high school grades, not their financial circumstances. Georgia no longer provides aid to kids because they are poor. Supporters of merit-based programs like these argue that they create incentives for students to work hard and do well in high school, and no doubt they do so. An unintended outcome of such programs, though, is that less aid goes to students with financial need. Students who are not near the top of their high school classes will get to some college if their families have money, but similarly performing students won't get there under these programs if their families are poor.

Although the trend in some states has been toward merit aid from the public sector, most of the merit aid now comes from the colleges themselves. Merit aid from colleges is really about attracting better students to that school than would otherwise come. Here colleges are price discriminating, even though the total amount of such aid is small. There is no doubt that schools today use merit aid to compete for higher-quality students, cutting the price to attract better students than would otherwise attend their college. Why are they interested in doing that? In part, it is because of the rise of prestige rankings like that of *U.S. News and World Report*, which ranks the desirability of schools. An important part of the rankings is the attributes of schools'

TABLE 4.2. Financial Aid Not Provided by the Feds

Type of Nonfederal Aid	% Who Get It	$ They Get
Athletic scholarship	0.85	10,000
Merit-based scholarship	8.00	7,100
Need-based from college	13.00	4,555
Private (nonschool)	8.00	3,400
Merit from state governments	4.00	2,770
From employer	5.50	4,200

Source: Post-Baccalaureate and Beyond Survey 2009 NCES, http://nces.ed
.gov/surveys/b&b/.

incoming classes—class rank in high school, SAT scores, and so
forth—as well as the percentage of students admitted who choose to
attend that school. A merit scholarship is a way to improve both scores.

Who gets that merit aid? If we define it broadly, some goes to athletes. As we can see in Table 4.2, it isn't a very big part of total aid, but
those who get it can get very big aid packages. Many parents hope that
their child will get to college on an athletic scholarship, but the actual
number of such scholarships is incredibly small. The number is regu-
lated by the National Collegiate Athletic Association (NCAA) depending on the size of the school and the athletic division in which it
participates. For example, Division I colleges are the largest schools
with the teams that appear regularly on television and undergraduate populations of 20,000 or more. They are allowed to have eighty-
five football scholarships—football is a sport with many players. But
they are allowed only four and a half tennis scholarships and none
for sports like rowing. In Division II, with smaller colleges, the number of scholarships falls sharply: only thirty-six for football, for
example. Women get an equal total number of scholarships, and
because they get none for football, which is the sport with the most
for men, they have more for other sports, twenty for rowing in Division I. These scholarships are a drop in the bucket compared to other
forms of aid.

The famous Ivy League is actually an athletic league bound together by a set of principles that effectively limit the role of sports on

campus. One of those principles is that there are no athletic scholarships on those campuses.

A lesson for parents is not to bet on your child getting an athletic scholarship. As a proportion of the student body, scholarships to play sports are microscopic, a couple of hundred among the 40,000 students in a big Division I school. Colleges may give preference in admissions to athletes even if they do not give them scholarships, of course.[7] But the idea that your high-school-athlete child is going to pay for college by playing sports is about as likely as a college player making it to the NBA or NFL.

Nor is it necessarily such a great thing for students if they do attend college on an athletic scholarship. It is a great deal of work to play competitive college sports, and then to maintain one's academic studies at the same time is an incredible challenge. If they stop playing, their scholarship typically ends, and whether they play depends on whether their coach wants them. That is why the National Labor Relations Board ruled that football players at Northwestern University (and presumably those at other schools as well) were effectively employees working at a job and eligible for the legal protections that employees have.[8] An encyclopedic study of the experiences of college athletes and their effect on campuses by James Shulman and former Princeton president William Bowen shows that the cultures of college sports programs and academic programs are often at odds. Student athletes seem to lose out a lot on the academic and other outside activities in college. They don't do as well in their classes, they don't participate as much in other extracurricular activities (with less time to do them), and they don't report having as good an experience in college as do nonathletes.[9] The chase to get athletic scholarships has become increasingly time and resource intensive. Colleges in some sports are now asking student athletes to commit to attend their school in the sophomore year of high school.

Parents may hope that their unique child will get a merit-based scholarship of some other kind, but nonathletic, merit-based scholarships are an even smaller part of the financial aid picture, especially at public institutions, where most students go. They are more common in private schools because those schools are more interested in competing for better students. It is true that colleges may well have a special place in their acceptance pool for students with unique attributes: Every college orchestra needs an oboe player, for example, and especially at smaller schools, colleges may have to make some effort to attract and admit students with those unique interests. (The best way to play that card is to talk directly to the coach, orchestra conductor, or campus official who runs that program and hope that person wants you to come enough to press the admissions staff for special consideration.) It would be extremely rare, though, for a college to give merit scholarships for extracurricular activities other than the limited athletic aid noted earlier.

Most merit scholarships come from colleges that want to attract students who they think might not come otherwise, typically students with better academic credentials because those factors matter so much to the school's rankings and prestige. The hard question for students and their families is whether they want to take the discount price offered through merit aid and go to a less selective school or pay more and go to a more elite school. Sometimes it works out that the school you want to attend is the one that gives you merit aid anyway. The job-market outcomes may not differ all that much between schools with similar programs, as we saw in the previous chapter, but schools may differ a lot in how much fun they are to attend and how well they fit the particular needs of a student.

Going to a school that may be less prestigious than others where you've been accepted is certainly worth thinking about, though, if the merit aid at that school is enough to avoid having to take on a lot of debt at the other schools or to keep your family from financial hardships. In terms of the return on the investment, making that move probably improves the return from a college education. Of course, if the student is miserable at a school where he or she didn't want to be, that's no fun either and is one of the big factors affecting whether students fail to finish college.

What do we know about how financial aid affects students? We might expect that students on financial aid would perform less well simply because they come from families with fewer resources to support education. Those students have done worse than students from wealthier families. My research with Shinjae Won found that students who received financial aid in the form of grants actually got better grades than did those from families with more means who did not get financial aid. But that positive effect was limited to those getting grants. Students getting work-study aid and loans did not do noticeably better or worse.[10]

There has been a long debate as to whether it helps students to work while in college, especially in getting a job after graduation. On the one hand, they are getting work experience, which as we saw earlier is what employers want. On the other hand, it is taking time and energy away from studies and other college activities—presumably the reason for being in college. As we saw earlier, most students are working while in college—almost two-thirds. The answer to whether working helps students depends on the type of work they are doing. Work that is related to their studies in some way does contribute to getting a better job when they graduate and getting a job sooner as compared to those who were working on tasks unrelated to their studies.[11] A work-study job may be the best bet for finding a job related to academic material, but remember that only one-third of students say that their work-study job has that relationship. For other students, work may be necessary, but it is a distraction.

Student Loans

The biggest issue in financial aid today is student debt from loans that were taken out to pay for college. Evidence suggests that loans are now the most common way that students are paying for college.[12]

Using loans to pay for college is an idea with great appeal to economists because the people getting the financial benefit—the graduates who get good jobs—are the ones paying for it, presumably in the future when they have those well-paying jobs. If there is not a good payoff from the degree, then that argument falls apart.

How good does the return have to be for loans to pay off? As we saw in the previous chapter, the rate of return on a college degree varies quite a bit, but the average rate seems to be about 7 percent per year—the big conclusion there is the huge variance in that rate across schools. That's not bad for an average, similar to the typical return from the U.S. stock market over time—except that a lot of student loans charge interest rates that are about the same. The average unsubsidized student loan, of the kind one might get directly from a college, has had an average interest rate of just under 7 percent since 2006. Those loans and the interest on them are not necessarily tax deductible, and the interest charges start from the day you take them out. College does not look very attractive in terms of the payoff under that scenario. The best rate, direct subsidized loans, have an interest rate set at 4.66 percent through June 2015, better but still not a slam dunk against the return on that investment.[13]

The more general problem with using loans to pay for college has to do with risk. Loans are best when one has a stable, well-paying job after college to pay them off. In an uncertain environment, loans are a very risky option because the interest on many loans continues to grow even if you don't have a job that allows you to pay them back. Students are rarely positioned to take on that risk. We need to get a bit further into the details of educational loans in the United States to assess what that risk means.

As we might expect, paying for college with student loans changes the decisions that students make along the way. One of the changes is that they are more likely to pursue degrees that lead to jobs in higher-paying fields and less likely to work in occupations like education or others that serve the public interest but that pay less.[14]

Most student loans originate with the federal government. The use of loans as a percentage of aid has actually declined since 2008 because the funding for grants has risen (the percentage of undergrads with subsidized loans from the federal government declined from 12 percent in 2007–2008 to 5 percent in 2012–2013). But the total amount of debt associated with loans has continued to grow, as Figure 4.3 shows.

Not surprisingly, student debt is higher for private schools because they cost more to attend. Of students borrowing, the average loan amount was $25,000 for students in public schools in 2012 versus $29,000 for those in private, nonprofit colleges. The rise in

FIGURE 4.3. Total Student Loan Balances by Age Group

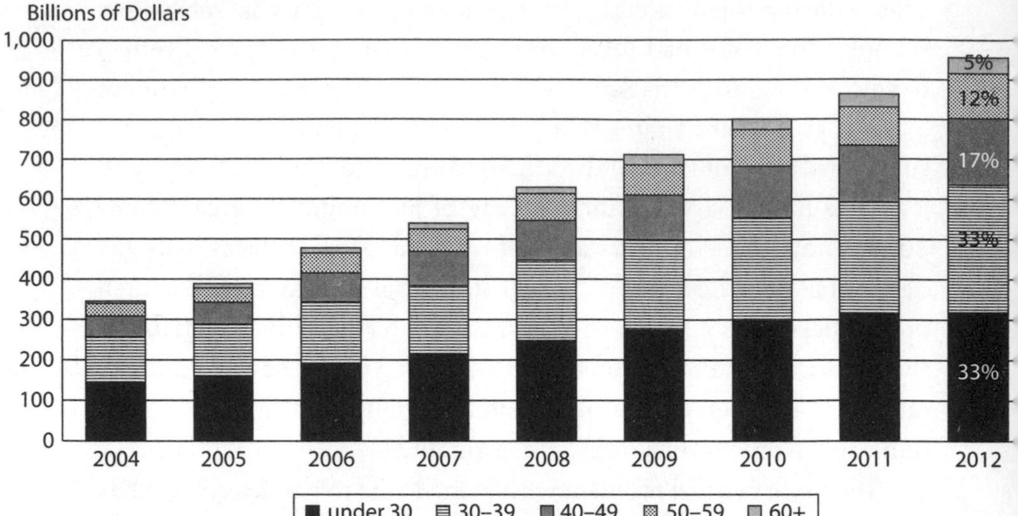

Billions of Dollars

Source: Andrew Haughwout, Donghoon Lee, Joelle Scally, and Wilbert van der Klaauw, *Measuring Student Debt and Its Performance* (Staff Report 668, Federal Reserve Bank of New York, April 2014), http://www.newyorkfed.org/research/staff_reports/sr668.pdf.

indebtedness is not because of more borrowing. It is because of the inability to pay off the debt, which causes debt to grow because the interest charges accumulate.

Figure 4.3 shows how the unpaid debt increased even before the Great Recession, doubling for graduates recently out of college between 2004 and 2008. While debts of other kinds declined in the population since the 2009 downturn, student loan debt increased—past credit card bills and now behind only mortgages as the largest source of debt in the United States.

The federal government now has a dizzying array of loan programs as well as an even more complicated set of repayment plans, some of which are tailored to the income of the graduate. Student loans are unique, though, in the difficulty in getting out from under them. It is possible to walk away from mortgage debt by turning your house over to the bank or to declare bankruptcy to get away from credit card and other forms of debt. There is nothing like that for student loans, however. Declaring personal bankruptcy does not eliminate the requirement to repay these loans. While the government

FIGURE 4.4. Loan Defaults by Type of College

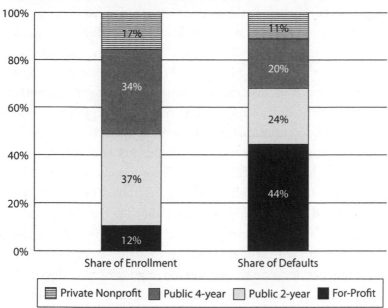

Source: U.S. Department of Education, IPEDS 12-month enrollment for 2012–2013 for schools in the fifty states plus Washington, DC, and FY 2011 three-year CDRs.

does have some arrangements to forgive loans, the requirements are very strict. (It is possible to apply to have loans forgiven if you die, for example.)[15] Loans have to be paid back even if you never graduate from college or if you never get a job in the field for which your degree prepared you. Typically interest accumulates if you fail to pay off the loan.

About 10 percent of those loans have been in default in recent years, and a larger number—around 17 percent—have been more than ninety days delinquent. The pattern of loan defaults in Figure 4.4 is revealing first in that graduates of the most expensive programs, the four-year private schools, actually have the lowest default rate.[16]

The highest default rate is for the new for-profit schools. Their programs are almost entirely vocational, designed with the sole purpose of getting students a job, but they haven't actually been good at doing that. The second-highest rate is for grads of community colleges, which are just behind the for-profits in having the most job-oriented programs. The *New York Times* has a very useful calculator that will tell you what the average loan amounts are for students at different colleges: http://www.nytimes.com/interactive/2014/your-money /student-loan-repayment-calculator.html. At Bowdoin College, for example, the average student debt is $22,755, and at the best government rate, you'll need an income of $31,760 to have a reasonable chance of being able to pay it off over the next ten years. The federal government will show you the default rate for any college at https://www.nslds.ed .gov/nslds_SA/defaultmanagement/search_cohort_3yr2011CY.cfm.

Overall, students have not been doing very well getting jobs that make it possible to pay off the loans. There is some evidence that the high level of student loan debt is holding back house buying for the next generation and, in turn, holding back growth of the economy.[17]

Deb Weinstein, a recent graduate, had some important insights into the problem with student loans in an article in *Forbes*, where she wrote about her decision to quit her job to go back to college in 2008, figuring that the recession would be an excellent time to be in school. She borrowed $50,000 to fund a one-year journalism degree, but when she graduated, there were no jobs and she owed over $1,800 per month in loans. She describes all the ways possible to at least avoid having the interest on the loans mount up until she can find a job. Staying on for more college would help but only for the federal loans. Interest on the others continues to pile up. In some cases, the military will pay off loans if it really needs your skills.

The most intriguing possibility is the income-based repayment program from the federal government, where you agree to pay a percentage of whatever you earn above a certain level for up to thirty years. That's a great deal if it turns out you are going to be broke for the next generation, not very good if it turns out you make some real money. (The income repayment program is pretty complicated. See https://studentloans.gov /myDirectLoan/mobile/repayment/repaymentEstimator.action for a calculator to estimate what you might owe using it.)[18]

The punch line about loans should be how very serious a commitment they involve. Most parents would cringe at the thought of their eighteen-year-old getting a mortgage for a house, but we give very little thought to him or her taking out big student loans, despite the fact that the loans represent a much more serious obligation. We know that graduating from college with a lot of debt affects career choices— law school grads who wanted to do advocacy work instead go to Wall Street firms, math grads who wanted to teach go to investment banks to make enough money to pay off their debts. Not being able to pay one's student loan debt ruins one's credit rating, which then inhibits other life options such as home ownership. By definition, students who get student loans do not have other financial resources to fall back on. Nor do their families, or they wouldn't have been eligible for loans in the first place.

A big caveat emptor about student loans is that they are not all the same, and the distinctions among them can be crucial.

- *Direct subsidized loans* are backed by the federal government. The amount of these loans is limited to financial need, and the government pays the interest on them while you are in school. There is a limit to how much you can borrow with this program over the course of an undergrad program—$23,000. That means full-time students cannot rely on these loans alone to cover the costs of their education.
- *Direct unsubsidized loans* are also backed by the federal government but not limited to those who demonstrate financial need. You pay the interest on these loans even while you are a student, and the interest rates are about two percentage points higher. There is a limit to how much you can borrow here as well. If you get the full $23,000 in subsidized loans, then you can add only $8,000 of unsubsidized loans.[19]
- *Private loans* can come from any lender and from the college itself. They are not backed by the government. Interest rates can fluctuate, and interest accrues all the time. Unlike direct loans, they are not tax deductible, and they may come with a series of onerous requirements. In some cases, a college granting these loans may withhold one's degree until the loan is paid off, which seems crazy—how do you pay off the loan if you can't get a job, and the degree is necessary to get a job? But it happens.

For many people, loans are the only way they can afford to go to college, and that makes a college education much more expensive and potentially risky as well. For those who have more choices, it is worth considering carefully whether a degree program that requires loans is really worth it. If the program requires you to take out unsubsidized loans, you should think very hard about doing it. If it requires private loans, you should have a long talk with someone who understands finance first. Think of these loans as being like car loans, except for most people they are much bigger, and unlike a car loan, you can't get out of your obligation to pay them off by giving the education back or by declaring bankruptcy. Because the limit on loans backed by the federal government is $31,000, the students you hear about who have borrowed $50,000 or even $100,000 to pay for their education are largely in debt to private lenders.

A reminder to parents: private loans often require a cosigner, and that would be you. The finance joke that there are two miracles in life—birth and compound interest—applies here because the miracle of compound interest drives the cost of these loans up a great deal over time. The interest rate even on some loans backed by the federal government is over 7 percent, so that means the interests costs would double the size of the loan in ten years.

For graduates who find themselves facing defaults because they are unable to pay for their loans, the immediate problem is almost always with private loans. The federal government's Consumer Financial Protection Bureau has had some pretty unpleasant things to say about how private lenders appear to have avoided trying to help people having trouble paying off these loans. It offers advice on how to deal with those lenders and to try to get help if you are struggling to pay off these loans.[20]

Schools vary considerably in the extent to which they use student loans in their financial aid packages. For-profit colleges use more than twice as much aid in the form of loans as do nonprofit schools, which is yet another reason why the return from those schools is so poor. The amount of aid in the form of loans also varies across selective schools, as we can see in Figure 4.5. NYU uses ten times as much aid

FIGURE 4.5. Borrowing to Credential Ratio at Elite Colleges, 2006–2009

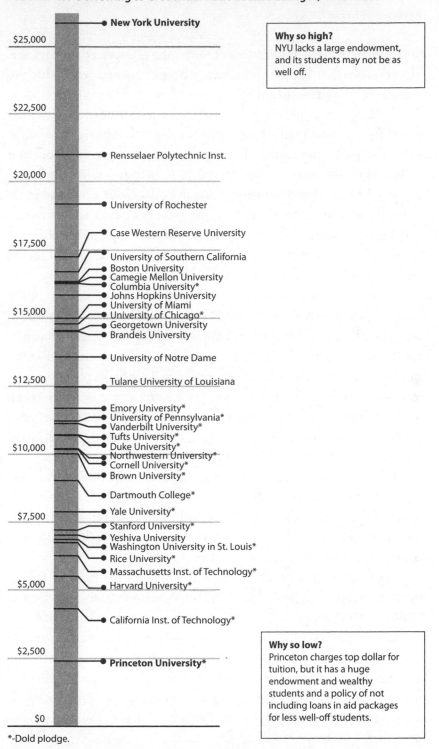

New York University

Why so high?
NYU lacks a large endowment, and its students may not be as well off.

$25,000

$22,500

$20,000 — Rensselaer Polytechnic Inst.

— University of Rochester

$17,500 — Case Western Reserve University

University of Southern California
Boston University
Carnegie Mellon University
Columbia University*
Johns Hopkins University
$15,000 — University of Miami
University of Chicago*
Georgetown University
Brandeis University

— University of Notre Dame

$12,500 — Tulane University of Louisiana

Emory University*
University of Pennsylvania*
Vanderbilt University*
Tufts University*
$10,000 — Duke University*
Northwestern University*
Cornell University*
Brown University*

— Dartmouth College*

$7,500 — Yale University*

Stanford University*
Yeshiva University
Washington University in St. Louis*
Rice University*
Massachusetts Inst. of Technology*
$5,000 — Harvard University*

— California Inst. of Technology*

$2,500 — **Princeton University***

Why so low?
Princeton charges top dollar for tuition, but it has a huge endowment and wealthy students and a policy of not including loans in aid packages for less well-off students.

$0

*-Dold pledge.

Sources: Analysis of undergraduate borrowing data obtained from the U.S. Department of Education for 2006–2007, 2007–2008, and 2008–2009, and the number of credentials awarded based on data from the Integrated Postsecondary Education Survey for 2006–2007, 2007–2008, and 2008–2009. Andrew Gillen, *In Debt and in the Dark: It's Time for Better Information on Student Loan Defaults*, n.d., Washington, DC. https://www.nslds.ed.gov/nslds _SA/defaultmanagement/search_cohort_3yr2011CY.cfm (accessed October 2014).

in the form of loans as does Princeton in the equivalent aid package. The reason is that Princeton has much deeper pockets from which to provide other sources of aid.

Given all this information about loans, the discussion about the payoff from college starts to have some real bite. Is it going to be worth going to a particular college if doing so means that you come out of it with tens of thousands of dollars in debt to private lenders, the interest on which has been building while in college, will continue to do after you graduate, and short of dying (which doesn't always work), bad life circumstances can't get you out of that obligation? You'd want to be very sure that there is a high payoff that is also pretty secure after graduation.

Table 4.3 tells us what most people really want to know, not the sticker price but what students and their parents are actually paying to send their kids to college, after financial aid. The "net price" column is the key one. Think of this as the equivalent of the *Consumer Reports* figures on what people actually pay for cars. The three columns represent the costs for public, private, and the new for-profit category of colleges, and the rows show sticker prices, aid packages, and the net price paid by income group. The figures do not include student loans, so the net price here is what students and their parents have to pay now.

Surprisingly, according to the College Board,[21] the average net cost of tuition and fees in 2013–2014 after financial aid was actually lower in real terms, discounting for inflation, than ten years before, although the fact that families are less able to pay for college now after the Great Recession may make that cold comfort.

What does all this aid work out to as a percentage of family income? Catharine Hill and Gordon Winston calculated that at Williams College, one of the more generous schools in terms of financial aid, the poorest fifth of families paid about 6 percent of their annual income for their child to attend Williams, while the richest fifth paid about 20 percent.[22] We can see here why financial aid is one of the few programs in society that gives poorer people a leg up, because at colleges like this one, they pay a smaller proportion of their income to send their kids to this college.

TABLE 4.3. Average Academic Year Cost of Attendance, Average Grant/Scholarship Aid, and Net Price of Attendance for Full-Time, First-Time Degree/Certificate-Seeking Undergraduate Students at Title IV Institutions, by Control of Institution, Level of Institution, and Other Selected Characteristics, United States, Academic Year 2011–2012

Level of institution, type of aid received, and family income level	Public			Private nonprofit			Private for-profit		
	Average cost	Average grant/ scholarship aid	Net price	Average cost	Average grant/ scholarship aid	Net price	Average cost	Average grant/ scholarship aid	Net price
Students receiving any grant aid	$18,258	$6,524	$11,734	$35,201	$14,566	$20,636	$26,986	$5,098	$21,888
Students receiving Title IV aid									
4-year									
All family income levels	18,304	5,770	12,534	35,190	14,682	20,508	26,880	4,517	22,363
$0–30,000	18,304	8,991	9,313	35,190	18,737	16,453	26,880	5,253	21,627
$30,001–48,000	18,304	7,612	10,692	35,190	18,363	16,827	26,880	4,654	22,226
$48,001–75,000	18,304	4,525	13,779	35,190	15,889	19,300	26,880	2,746	24,134
$75,001–110,000	18,304	2,277	16,027	35,190	13,838	21,352	26,880	1,167	25,713
$110,001 and more	18,304	1,690	16,614	35,190	11,156	24,034	26,880	1,216	25,663

Source: NCES.

Table 4.2 reveals something important about the new for-profit schools. Despite having a lower sticker price than private schools, for-profit schools have a higher net price because there is less aid available. This is a good reminder that the sticker price is not the most important figure to consider. A second point is that even students from families that are not poor get some aid from private schools, enough to cover about one-third of college costs. The College Board calculates that students in the bottom 25 percent of the family income distribution now pay essentially no tuition and fees at four-year public schools. In terms of the rate of return, that makes it almost a sure thing for those students to go to college.

A third point is that because of financial aid, the cost difference between private and public colleges is not as great as many people think. That difference was $9,000 per year for the average student receiving some aid—need or merit based.

Many readers are no doubt wondering how the average sticker price of going to a private college before financial aid could be only $35,000 per year, as the table indicates, when they read about tuition alone being north of $50,000 at many private schools. It is a good reminder of how much variation there is in the cost of going to college in the United States. There are many private schools that keep tuition costs very low, some out of principle, such as Rice University, some by necessity because the demand for spaces at their school is low.

There is lots of variation in financial aid across private colleges, on the basis largely of how rich they are. Superelite colleges do have super sticker prices, but those colleges like Harvard, Penn, Princeton, and Yale have also pledged enough financial aid so that students whose families have income below $100,000 per year—the top income category in Table 4.2—will be charged nothing to attend. Even if it doesn't matter much to go to an elite school for your career after, an issue we consider in the next chapter, it might matter a lot in terms of financial aid.

The College Navigator website from the Department of Education will give average data on the amount of aid each college gives students by categories of family income. That may not tell you all that much about your own case, however, as so many other factors matter to financial aid decisions, such as financial assets, number of children in the family, and so forth. The private website CollegeData.com breaks out that data in a way that might be easier to understand.

The *New York Times* columnist Ron Lieber reports that the average family applying for financial aid in a large cohort of private colleges is now earning more than $100,000. He also notes that it is possible to appeal financial aid decisions, at least those based on need, and that as many as 50 percent of appeals are successful. Some schools such as Cornell University will match need-based aid packages from other colleges where an applicant has been accepted.[23] Colleges, however, are unlikely to match merit aid. They've already calculated how much it is worth to them to have you come, and if you are worth more to someone else, so be it. It's strictly business. (For those who want to check up on the financial aid package they've been offered and whether they have gotten everything that at least the federal government authorizes, https://www.nslds.ed.gov/nslds_SA/ will let you know. It helps to be comfortable with acronyms for government programs. The software requires that you have already applied for financial aid before you can use it. The advantage is that with the appropriate code, which you are given when you apply for financial aid at a college, the software already knows most everything about you, which makes it easier if not necessarily comforting.)

Does It Help Your Admission Chances Not to Apply for Financial Aid?

Many parents suspect that their child will have a better chance of being accepted to a college if their child is not applying for financial aid. These tend to be the people who think that colleges really operate like businesses and will do what they can to make money, including making admission decisions that save them from paying aid. Are they right?

Sort of. Colleges typically deny that the need for financial aid affects the chances of getting in, and many of them still have something of a wall between the admissions decision and the financial aid decision. The latter happens only after students have been admitted.

However, a recent survey of admissions directors reports otherwise. Forty-one percent of the directors in private colleges report that they are held accountable for the percentage of "full-pay" students admitted. In other words, their college wants that number up and rewards the administrators for doing so. In state and public universities, the figure is much lower—25 percent—but you can bet that all colleges must track the full-pay admissions if they care about their budgets.[24] A study of the University of Oregon found that the administration had a fair amount of discretion in using financial aid to influence which admitted students ended up coming to campus.[25]

What's the advice here? It would be crazy not to apply for financial aid if you have a good chance to get some, simply to hope that it will allow you to get into a more selective school. The really elite college are likely to be those where financial aid doesn't influence admissions decisions, and as we saw earlier, going to a more selective college may have little impact on the long-run return from college. But if you are sure there is no way you are eligible for financial aid, it's not a bad idea to make that clear when applying.

Thinking about the incentives that drive a school is generally a smart thing to do, though. The most important of these on the admissions side is schools' interest in getting lots of students to apply, so that they can turn a lot of them down and be more selective in the rankings, and their interest in having the students they accept come, which makes them more desirable in those same rankings. The fact that colleges encourage you to apply does not mean that they necessarily think that you have a good chance of being admitted. If you can assure them that you will come, though, they are more likely to take you, which is why acceptance rates are higher for early admission decisions, where students have to make that promise.

5

Getting That First Job After College

DESPITE THE FACT that the costs of college can't really be known until after we learn about financial aid decisions and that they vary college by college, the cost side of the return-on-investment equation is much easier to understand than what the payoff will be. That latter piece of evidence is so much harder to know because it requires trying to guess what jobs will be available at graduation and how well they will pay.

The college-to-job transition is something like a messy supply chain, and the end point that is pulling the whole relationship along is employers. Students and their parents are trying to guess what employers will want to hire when those students graduate years later, colleges are at least trying to guess what parents and students think employers will want to hire, and the fact that employers are now expecting graduates to have job skills before they arrive has altered expectations dramatically. So everything is pointing toward employers.

What is it that they want? Many observers and especially those with a bent toward public policy seem to attribute magical abilities to employers, especially businesses. They think that employers have worked out the optimal strategy for everything, that they have figured out exactly the skill sets that pay off, which students have them, and how much those students are worth. In fact, employers are just people. They have the same biases and limitations as everyone else. Not everything they do makes sense even in terms of their own self-interest.

Figuring out what predicts which candidates will turn out to be good employees is very tricky because it requires first being able to identify the job performance of employees in a standard and accurate way. That may be straightforward for a few jobs, such as sales consultants, but for most jobs, it requires a lot of time and effort. (How accurate do you think the performance appraisals are at the place you work?) Second, someone has to do the statistical analysis that compares the attributes of candidates before they were hired to job performance after. Third, the organization then has to take the lessons from that analysis and make hiring managers follow them. This has to be done separately for each job.

Some companies are pretty sophisticated about hiring, as you would imagine they are at the big operations like IBM or Google that hire a lot of people. In part because employees don't have lifetime careers anymore, hiring doesn't seem to be as big a priority for U.S. employers as it was a generation ago, when candidates would be assessed for weeks before being hired. Companies have cut so much of their human resource staff and budgets that they don't have the resources to do these analyses, nor does human resources necessarily have the political clout to make hiring managers do things in a standardized manner. It is now quite likely that hiring decisions are heavily influenced, if not outright driven, by an executive who has no training in human resources and no real data on whether his or her hiring practices are working or not. The smaller the company, the more likely that is to be the case. It's very common for a company to choose a particular college for recruiting because that's where the CEO went and to rely on hiring methods that have been shown to be particularly poor predictors of good hires, such as having candidates interviewed by one manager after another and then asking the managers what they think.

Many people—especially pundits in the business press—seem to have what I've called the Home Depot view of the hiring process: Filling a job vacancy is like replacing a part in a washing machine. We go down to the store to get that part, and once we find it, we put it in place and get the machine going again. Like a replacement part, job requirements are very precise. Job candidates must fit them perfectly, or the job won't be filled and the business can't operate. When employers have vacancies, it must mean that there is no one available who could do the job. So the trick for students is just to figure out what those vacancies require and go get the skills to do them.

That is simply not the way jobs and hiring works. I describe how hiring works today in my book *Why Good People Can't Get Jobs*.[1] The most important difference between reality and the Home Depot model is that, unlike a machine part, no perfect fit exists between applicants and job requirements. Put another way, the same tasks can be performed in lots of different ways. The National Institute for Economic and Social Research in London did a series of fascinating studies looking at how companies making almost identical products but operating in different countries got their work done. It found, for example, that U.S. operations used more engineers and more unskilled workers, while German firms used more skilled craftspeople and fewer engineers and unskilled workers to perform the same business tasks. How the companies made the choices that drove those differences is something we return to later.[2]

Nor do job requirements remain constant. When candidates for a particular job are scarce and expensive, employers reduce job requirements. They are willing to hire applicants with lower skills to fill the job without driving their wages up. When demand is down and applicants are plentiful, job requirements rise as employers expect more qualifications before they hire someone.[3] During the information technology (IT) job boom of the 1990s, for example, only about 10 percent of the people working in real IT jobs had any kind of IT academic qualifications, no doubt because finding people with such qualifications was difficult and very expensive. The reverse is true when there are many more applicants than jobs.

The Home Depot view might also suggest that once employers find the right candidate, they hire that person and pay the wage necessary for that job. Supply and demand are equalized through prices, so there should be a clear market wage for each job. Software engineers may be expensive, but if you are willing to raise your wages high enough, you can get them.[4]

In the real world, though, employers do not act this way. Candidates, as noted earlier, are not identical, and the jobs can be performed in different ways by individuals with different attributes. Thus, if we shop around sufficiently, we should be able to find someone willing to do the job at a lower wage or someone who is able to perform the job at a higher standard for the same wage. In more formal terms, employers search. They put in the time and effort to find out what the candidates are like, and they wait to make a hiring decision until that information is safely in hand.

Not surprisingly, we spend more effort searching when we think it will pay off and also when it is easier to do so. If only one store in town is selling something we need, we are likely to just go there and buy it. If dozens of shops are vying for our trade, we are more likely to look around. If we find lots of variation in prices and in the characteristics of those items, we spend more time searching because we feel we are more likely to find a deal.

Employers may take a while to fill vacancies not because no one fits but precisely because there are *so many* qualified applicants. It might well pay off to just wait and see if someone will take this job who is just perfect for it, not merely qualified, or even wait to see who will do the job at a wage well below the market rate. This situation is not unlike teenagers who think they have many possible dates for the prom putting off asking anyone in particular while considering their options. Employers, too, can be so dazzled by the choices that they wait too long to fill jobs, especially because they cannot easily see the costs of not filling them. Pundits contend that the existence of vacancies proves something must be wrong with the possible candidates or the jobs would have been filled. That's just not true.

Especially when there are so many applicants, hiring managers find it hard to resist including in job descriptions the experiences and skills that will ensure that a successful candidate can step right into the job and do everything needed. Especially with the abundance of talent looking for jobs, why not? Law firms, for example, now routinely require bachelor's degrees for legal secretary jobs despite the fact that until recently those jobs were typically filled by high school grads. There is no evidence that the job requires a college degree, but if you can get them at the going wage, the argument goes, it can't hurt and it might help. Cost cutting means that there are fewer recruiters pushing back to question whether those requirements are necessary, and so we also get requirements that are impossible to fill, like the joke Silicon Valley job advert: "Must have five years' experience in a programming language that doesn't exist yet."

A job that a few years earlier was filled by new college graduates now requires several years of experience, ruling out today's new grads. New this generation is the rise of computerized applicant tracking systems that scan résumés to sort out qualified candidates. Job requirements are now built into hiring software that screens applications so that new college grads have no opportunity to persuade a recruiter that they could do the job. Once each requirement is in the software, whether it is critical or trivial, it essentially becomes something like a hurdle that applicants have to clear to become a qualified candidate.

As with all administrative processes, some of those requirements can be astoundingly stupid. A Wharton student we heard from had been ruled unqualified for a particular job because the job required a business degree and the diploma from the Wharton School is actually a bachelor's in applied economics. Despite the fact that Wharton is the oldest business school in the world and invented business education, a Wharton degree apparently didn't count as a business degree. A human resources manager told me there were 25,000 applicants for a reasonably standard engineering job and that none of them had been rated as qualified for the job by the applicant tracking software. The experience of having an application handled by applicant tracking software is typically quite discouraging—there is rarely, if any, follow-up on what is happening with the application—so much so that the consistent advice from job-search experts is to avoid it altogether and do whatever it takes to talk to a real person.

Nor is it the case that employers are necessarily in a hurry to fill vacancies even if they find good candidates. The first and most practical difference between the Home Depot view and the reality of hiring is that unlike the need to replace parts to keep a machine running, jobs don't necessarily have to be filled to keep an organization going. Employers operate with vacancies all the time. In some cases, the work gets done by other people who cover the tasks required in the vacant job. In others, the tasks get delayed, or temps and other help are brought in until the job gets filled. In fact, it saves money, at least in the short run, not to fill vacancies.

The problems facing college grads seeking jobs since 2008 have been exacerbated by the oversupply of talent that continues to linger after the Great Recession and the fact that employers just have too many applicants who under more typical circumstances could do the job. Many of those problems will get better when the economy improves, but even tight labor markets may not solve all the difficulties facing new entrants.

Most hiring does take place to replace turnover in existing jobs. While the annual turnover rate in the United States changes a lot depending on how strong the economy is, the consensus now is that it is much higher than in previous generations, especially for better-paid positions. So there must be more hiring. Is that good news for graduates?

Unfortunately, no, because most employers looking to hire someone who leaves want candidates who don't need to be trained, which pulls employees out of some other organization, creating turnover there. The fact that employees do leave, however, is one of the justifications for not training new hires—if we invest in them, they will just leave. That creates the Catch-22 of the labor market for college grads: You need experience to get a job, but nobody wants to give you experience.

None of this suggests that employers are bad. Hiring is a very difficult task, and they are typically trying to manage it with insufficient resources. Many of the challenges are beyond the control of any individual employer, such as the fact that turnover is up. Biases and lack of information come into play here as in every other aspect of life. The conclusion is just that we shouldn't expect a simple, logical, and consistent approach to hiring across all employers.

Poaching in the World of Banking

Nowhere is the reluctance to hire young people right out of college greater than in the world of hedge funds, which routinely top the list of having the highest paid executives on the planet. Even though hedge funds are after the same kind of young talent that investment banks want, the hedge funds rarely follow their banking colleagues to college campuses to recruit. Instead, they wait for the investment banks to hire fresh grads. Then the hedge funds hire the young employees away from the investment banks. That part is not so surprising. What is stunning is how some of them do it. They often grab the new bankers after only a few months on the job, but they don't take them away yet. They cut confidential deals with the new bankers to have them stay at the investment bank and keep learning for a year or more and then leave for the hedge fund, getting as much out of their current employer as possible. In a sense, this is like buying an option on an employee that will come due in a year or so. Given that they are hedge funds, perhaps this isn't such a surprise.

What Do Employers Want?

But surely someone is hiring graduates. What do those employers want?

In some parts of the economy, things haven't changed much for new graduates. Elementary and secondary schools are still looking for recent college graduates to teach K–12 students. Government functions like police and fire prevention have academies and training for school leavers. The big changes—and most of the jobs—are in the private sector.

There are over six million private employers in the United States, and they employ about three-fourths of the labor force in the country. About half of employees work in firms with over five hundred employees, where we might expect some reasonably standard and sophisticated employment practices. About one in six work in good-size businesses (one hundred to five hundred employees), about one in six work in small companies (twenty to one hundred employees), and the rest work in small businesses where practices are pretty informal.[5] In fact, those businesses are small enough to be exempt from a lot of government regulations governing hiring.

Given that diversity and the fact that those six million firms are spread across industries as well as large regions, it is no surprise that they do not speak with one voice. Nor do they all have the same interest in hiring. Figuring out what they want is tricky in part because it is quite different depending on which industry and what employers we are talking about and because, as noted earlier, they typically don't know what they need until just before they need it.

That has not stopped associations, journalists, commentators of all kinds, and the government itself from offering pronouncements about what employers need and will need in the future. Those pronouncements don't matter much to the employers, but they matter a lot to job seekers and even more to students and their parents who are trying to position themselves for the future labor market.

Most of those forecasts have focused on science and engineering jobs, and they tend to be wrong.[6] The Cold War and the National Defense Education Act of 1958 helped make the pursuit of science and engineering education in college patriotic, part of the effort to compete with and beat the Soviet Union, which at the time was ahead of us in the space race. Although complaints by employers about shortfalls of graduates in these areas were often common, virtually all the serious reports on science and technology jobs found a surplus of qualified people. A common manifestation of the surplus is postdoctoral programs, where graduates park for a few years—essentially cheap labor for more senior researchers—because there are not enough regular jobs to go to.

In the early 1990s, the complaints about inadequate education shifted to high schools. The 1983 report *A Nation at Risk*[7] highlighted declines in student achievement of all kinds in the 1970s and helped cement in the mind of the public for decades after that U.S. schools were failing. Not everyone made that argument, however. An equally attention-getting report a few years later by the Carnegie-funded National Center on Education and the Economy, *America's Choice: High Skills or Low Wages?*,[8] argued that while employers were not currently facing any skill problems, they needed to transform the way they operated, and higher skills were needed to do that. The U.S. Secretary of Labor put that idea in motion with a new commission that envisioned a future when workplaces had moved toward high-performance work systems that required greater skills. The report's recommendations called for a generic set of skills from all high schools, including basic skills (reading, writing, math, etc.), thinking skills such as decision making, and personal attributes such as responsibility. Developed in the Republican George H. W. Bush administration, these ideas were nevertheless embraced by the Democratic Bill Clinton administration and dominated the discussion of skills throughout the 1990s.

The most important outcome in this period was driven by those reports, and that was the school-to-work movement, which asserted that the way to improve students' skills and to increase their employability for jobs was to bring school and employers closer together. In practice, that meant apprenticeships, co-op programs, internships, and other arrangements that would help students see the practical value of classroom lessons, using business and workplace examples in the classroom and also seeing how those examples could be applied at work. The School-to-Work Opportunities Act of 1994 provided administrative and financial support to help build those connections.

Employers seemed to connect with schools in the late 1990s, no doubt because the low rate of unemployment made finding new talent before competitors could hire them a priority. Sixty-four percent of schools reported that they had at least one school-to-work program (the most popular of which was "job shadowing"), and 38 percent of students participated in one of those programs. Seventy-one percent of for-profit establishments—the local operations—reported that they were involved in some school-to-work program with their local schools.[9] In contemporary terms, these are remarkably high levels of involvement. As a result, it was possible for a high school student while still in school to connect with an employer that would provide some training and skills and, eventually, a job.

Arrangements for connecting employers and students make even more sense at the college level, where there is a much greater diversity of knowledge among students and therefore more overlap with employers' interests. These arrangements could actually create value for the employers.

The School-to-Work Act expired in 1999, a new administration came to Washington in 2001 with less interest in a role for government in business, and the recession of 2001 combined to end most of those programs. The idea that employers should have an important role in upgrading the skills of the workforce seemed to die with them as the need for new graduates eroded. But it was not because of any evidence suggesting that these programs weren't a good idea. They still seem to be the best bet for getting employers the skills they need and helping students learn how to apply academic material.

The skills-related arguments that followed came from consultants who asserted that in the near future there would simply not be enough people to meet labor demand. The fact that unemployment at the time was high and that, with the possible exception of World War II, the United States has never had a labor shortage did not seem to matter. Those arguments were kicked off by McKinsey & Company's "The War for Talent" study,[10] which saw the smaller "baby bust" age cohort born in the 1970s and claimed that this would soon cause a shortfall in middle-aged employee talent. Why there would be any need for middle-age talent was not clear, and the shortage did not come to pass. But similar reports followed, such as one from the U.S. Chamber of Commerce,[11] which assumed that the impending retirement of the baby boom cohort would lead to an absolute decline in the size of the labor force and, as they saw it, a severe worker shortage.

These arguments seem to be based on a simple misreading of the facts about U.S. labor supply. The U.S. population and the labor force did not decline because of the "baby bust" cohort and won't when the baby boomers retire. We know this with certainty because the next generation of workers has already been born! We know when they will leave school and become workers. None of these labor-shortage claims have turned out to be right, of course, and the new ones that predict shortages by 2015 aren't going to be right either. Why do people continue to make them? Sometimes they just don't understand what they are saying, but the claims also get attention, which is not a bad thing for the authors—and few people remember when the claims turn out to be wrong.

A similar set of complaints is that even if there is no shortage of labor, there are shortages of skilled labor. The President's Council on Jobs and Competitiveness,[12] a business-led council (twenty of its twenty-four members were from business), claimed that the United States would have a shortfall of 1.5 million college graduates by 2020, while others claim that the supply of college graduates in the United States will fall short by as many as 3 million individuals by 2018.[13] To put that figure in perspective, it is like saying that the economy needs almost twice as many four-year college graduates as will leave school this year. That would be amazing.

There are many problems with these claims, one of which is that they assume that every job held by a college graduate requires a college degree now and will require one in the future, denying the issue of overqualification. But we know that overeducation is widespread. The average U.S. worker has about 30 percent more education than his or her current job requires, and that figure has been rising over time. About 60 percent of parking-lot attendants, for example, have at least some college education. While it might be nice to discuss political science with your parking-lot valet, it isn't really a requirement of the job.

Another argument is that new technology is going to require that workers have more skills. There is at least some anecdotal evidence that some kinds of technology have eliminated the simplest tasks in jobs that used to be the preserve of new hires. Compiling performance and accounting data, for example, used to be the preserve of entry-level management jobs and their counterparts in the accounting industry as it required relatively little advanced knowledge. But enterprise-wide software systems and more sophisticated software have automated those tasks, eliminating them as a means for new hires to make contributions without much experience.[14]

Are job requirements actually going up? An interesting study compared the job requirements across the U.S. economy in the 1970s to those today. The requirements have indeed increased over the past forty or so years, but the changes are very modest: "academic skills" (analytic, quantitative, and verbal) up only 4 percent; computer skill requirements up 8 percent, surprisingly small given the dramatic increase in the use of computers; and especially relevant for the STEM skills debate, no increase in science and engineering skill requirements.

Despite that evidence, the more common claim now is that we need lots more grads with STEM degrees. These complaints have come and gone in the past, but they became more intense when new IT companies like Microsoft joined the group disturbed by the shortages. The public dispute over whether there was any shortfall in the supply of IT workers began with a fight between the U.S. Department of Commerce, which argued, based on information from employers, that there was a serious shortfall and that we needed more foreign workers to meet the need, and the Government Accounting Office, which disagreed, questioning the evidence presented in the Department of Commerce's argument. There is a lot of money at stake in this argument and so, of course, a lot of lobbying and politics.

The evidence for recent grads suggests clearly that there is no overall shortage of STEM grads. For example, only 22 percent of graduates with degrees in science and math got jobs using those skills. Half the engineering grads took jobs in fields other than engineering, with about 30 percent of those saying that they could not find a job in engineering and another 30 percent saying that the engineering jobs available were not as attractive as those in other fields.[15]

Whether employers need more IT and engineering grads—there just is no evidence at all of a greater need for science and math grads—depends on what you think "need" means. If it means that it isn't possible to get the work done with the applicants who are currently available, then the doubters are surely right. If it means that employers would like to hire more graduates in these fields of the quality they are currently hiring at the wages they are currently paying, then the employer groups are surely right.

Since 2000–2001, students have shifted their majors toward STEM degrees so that the number of STEM grads has increased faster than the overall number of bachelor's degrees.[16] Whether there will be jobs for these STEM grads when they graduate is another story, as the evidence just presented suggests that the demand is not really there now.

The efforts to press public universities and colleges to turn out more students in the fields that employers say they want, under consideration in the Texas and Florida legislatures, among others, is a fool's errand. Even if schools could compel or incentivize students to pursue certain majors, trying to predict what will be hot in the labor market several years in the future is almost impossible. No school (and no legislator, if he or she thought about it) wants to explain to angry parents why the degree the school pushed, their child worked several years to get, and they spent a great deal of money to support ended up leading nowhere.

How could there be so much noise about the need for STEM graduates if there really aren't jobs for them? A possible explanation is that even though there are not so many jobs for these grads, the new hires don't stay in them very long, and when they leave those jobs, they leave science and engineering careers altogether. We need lots of STEM grads to make up for the fact that we can't keep them in their fields. In 2001, for example, which was the peak of the dot-com IT boom and the best labor market in thirty years, only 29 percent of graduates with science and engineering degrees had science and engineering jobs two years later. About half of computer science engineers and electrical engineers have left those fields for other careers after ten years. The most common reasons they left was because the work was more interesting in other fields and there were better opportunities elsewhere. My own look at the IT field in the booming 1990s found that the biggest single issue affecting the supply of talent in those occupations was that people left them in droves after just a few years. The lack of career prospects appeared to be an important factor.[17]

Why does turnover out of these fields matter for a college student? Because it indicates that there is something different in these entry-level jobs that may not lead to long-term careers. Employers may have lots of job openings in entry-level engineering and IT because they can't keep people in those fields, so they keep having to hire people in the front door because they are losing them out the back door. That may lead to very attractive entry-level jobs, but it also means that there may be no long-term future in those jobs. For those who wonder why more students don't go into these fields and instead still pack business programs, the most popular major, a good guess might be that business degrees continue to be useful for a long time, and careers in business have the potential to last a lifetime. Business schools teach how to calculate long-run rates of return on investments for a reason.

The fact that employers seem to be saying that they have a greater need for science skills yet the jobs don't seem to be there suggests that maybe a different kind of degree is in order. The Alfred P. Sloan Foundation helped fund the Professional Science Master's initiative that has a stronger orientation to the use of the science and some training in organizational skills. In structure, the degree looks much like an undergraduate co-op program in that the idea is to develop the content with input from employers and for the employers to provide workplace experiences in which the classroom content will be used. There are about two hundred of these degree programs now in the United States, mostly at regional state colleges. As with the School-to-Work movement for high school students a generation ago, there is a broad consensus that programs like this are the best bet for connecting classroom learning to workforce skills. (For a complete list of the programs, see http://www.sciencemasters.com.)

Let's Ask the Employers!

One of the troubling things about most of the reports about college students and jobs is that few of them ever ask the people who are actually hiring students what it is they want. When we do, the answers are surprising, shocking really if you think college classrooms are the place to learn job skills.

What employers that are actually doing the hiring complain about in new graduates has been consistent for decades, and that is attitudes in the workplace. Mainly this is a concern about conscientiousness: Can they show up on time? Will they try even when tasks are difficult? Can they take direction? and so forth. Psychologists have been inclined to see behaviors like these as being rooted in dispositions, but recent arguments suggest that they can be taught. Complaints about shortfalls in specific academic skills have always been quite rare. It is behaviors associated with maturity that are the overwhelming issue, not surprising given that the workers we are talking about are not very old or mature yet.[18]

When employers do hire from college, academic skills (as noted earlier) are not an important concern. A survey of employers conducted by the National Association of Colleges and Employers, asking about specific abilities and skills that employers valued in new college hires, found something similar, that "technical knowledge related to the job" (vocational skills like hospitality management) was ranked sixth out of nine attributes.[19] They valued skills that could be learned in any serious degree program, such as the abilities to make decisions, to communicate, and to process information. But even these skills are not as important as work experience. A similar survey of employers conducted by the *Chronicle of Education* (2013) of attributes of new hires shows that work experience is the crucial attribute that employers want; and remember, *this is for students who may not have had a full-time job yet.* The relevance of course work to the job in question is just not that important (see Figure 5.1).

Employers say that having internships trumps your college major—by a lot—as does the nature of any noninternship, by definition part-time job you had in college. Unpaid, volunteer experiences outside the classroom are almost as important as the college major, and extracurricular activities, such as being in the French club, are just about as important.

It probably will take a minute or two for the point to sink in, but while colleges are promising that very vocational majors like health

FIGURE 5.1. Relative Importance of Attributes in Evaluating Graduates for Hire

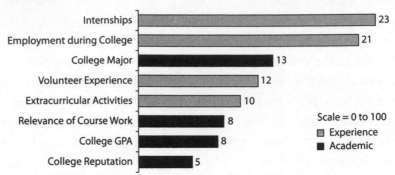

Source: *Chronicle of Higher Education*, "The Role of Higher Education in Career Development: Employer Perceptions," 2012, http://chronicle.com/items/biz/pdf /Employers%20Survey.pdf

care software administration are the key to good jobs, and students are shifting toward them, the employers may not care much about them.

The relative lack of value that employers actually place on the academic component of the college experience is demonstrated by stunning evidence in the same survey showing that even for jobs that are said to require a college degree, 70 percent of employers would ignore that requirement altogether if other characteristics of the candidate were a good fit. If that many employers would ignore something that is a requirement for a job, it suggests that the requirement may be more of a proxy for things that are hard to observe but that could be measured some other way. If employers can see those things directly, as evidenced by success in a job, then the college degree is just not that relevant. What they want to see is work experience, and that is hard to observe for new graduates.

Another reason why work experience matters is because most employers don't want to spend the time or money to give new hires the initial skills one learns in any first job—how to handle yourself at work—and the more focused job skills learned early on in a specific job. The consulting firm Accenture's 2013 survey of employers re-ported a third of them admitting that any problems they were having finding the right candidates stemmed from not providing enough training for them. They try to get around the lack of training by find-ing candidates who already have it.

The survey also offers evidence about the primary assertion behind the move toward more vocational college programs, that there is an unmet demand for colleges to provide job skills. The employers say that the biggest shortfalls are in managing priorities, decision mak-ing, organization and planning skills, and in oral and written commu-nication. (See Appendix for the outcomes.) None of these skills have anything to do with occupation-specific courses.

There is no perceived gap in "technical skills associated with the job" and "knowledge of a content area associated with the job." These are the job-specific skills one might think could require a specialized degree. Students are actually rated as overqualified on analytic and research skills. There is no need, according to these data, for students to know more about the fields in which they are applying for jobs. The gaps are in areas that we might think of as life skills.

These results from actual employers don't say that college is irrel-evant. What they say is that the job skills part doesn't matter. College experience seems to be used as a proxy for other attributes, but em-ployers would rather see those attributes directly in the form of suc-cessful work experience.

What does this say about pursuing a specialized, vocational de-gree, something designed with the goal of getting a job in a particular industry or in a particular job function, like pharmaceutical market-ing? It doesn't sound encouraging because it doesn't seem necessary, and specialized degrees have the downside of locking you into a career that may not be ideal.

The economist Ofer Malamud examined whether specializing early on helps or hurts one's future career with the interesting com-parison of the education systems in England, where students pick a subject area when they apply for college and focus only on that field, and Scotland, where college students pursue general courses in their first two years of college before specializing. He finds more English grads switching to careers that are substantially different from their college training than do their Scottish peers. Presumably the first career proved not to be such a good bet. When the English grads switch careers, they pay a bigger price in terms of wage penalty than do those from Scottish colleges.[20] In other words, there are big risks associated with specializing that come with costs.

The implications from a study of vocational education may also offer some lessons for the job focus of many college programs. High school students with strong practical training that pointed them toward a specific job appear to do better in their first job out of school than do students with a more general educational program, but those advantages dissipate over time. The more vocational backgrounds made it more difficult to change career paths and adapt in general to new workplace realities that inevitably occur later in life.[21]

One of the issues with these practical, vocational courses is what you could have been learning instead. A class that teaches students the government regulations that apply in a field like health care might be of some real interest to a health care employer who is hiring that year; but that knowledge is not going to be useful for long, and the student could have been in classes that provided general, lifelong lessons, such as learning how to make better decisions or to better understand other people. The evidence just presented seems to imply that grads from job-focused programs missed out on something in their course work that hurt them after their first job.

The Internship Problem

It certainly seems as though the best thing that a college student interested in getting a job can do is get work experience. How do you get experience if it is required in order to get a job in the first place, and how do you do that if you're still in college?

One answer is internships. That's what employers want. Internships also provide a solution to the apparent conundrum of otherwise expecting college classrooms to provide work-based experiences and skills: Get that experience elsewhere

The *Economist* magazine recently offered an international review of internship programs, which seem to be expanding around the world. The European Union's Commission in Brussels brings in 1,500 interns at a time; the China phenomenon Alibaba has an international program of internships, as does Infosys in Bangalore; entire industries like fashion and journalism seem to rest on unpaid interns. The United States still seems to be the mother lode of internships in part because such a high percentage of them here are free. The *Economist* estimates that 90 percent of U.S. colleges give academic credit for internships, which allows the employers to qualify those experiences as unpaid and also allows the college to give academic credit (which the students and their families are paying for) for something that the college doesn't itself have to deliver. We consider the cost issue later.[22]

Increasingly employers seem to be using internships as a means of screening candidates for job offers. At Penn, for example, 180 employers now come to campus to hire interns for the summer, and 87 percent of graduates in 2014 had reported having an internship. Figure 5.2, from the *Economist*, uses data from LinkedIn members to report whether internships led to full-time job offers. The extent to which they do, especially in fields like accounting, means that the job-search process moves up even earlier in the college experience, given that internship offers are extended during the junior year for that summer.

Not all companies use internships to hire, and there are lots more students looking for internships than there are openings. When companies aren't hiring, the internships they do have tend to go away.

Into this gap have come unpaid internships. What are they? There is a big difference between what they are *supposed* to be and what they in fact are. Unpaid internships at for-profit firms are supposed to be strictly for the benefit of the intern. The employer is not supposed to get any benefit out of them. If that is not the case, the interns are supposed to be paid, according to the Fair Labor Standards Act. In practice, though, there is often very little difference between paid and unpaid internships except for the lack of money in the latter. In fields like

FIGURE 5.2. Internal Combustion: Internships
That Lead to Jobs (Percentage of Total, 2013)

	0	10	20	30	40	50	60	Internships per 1,000 people hired
Accounting								49
Oil & energy								20
Investment banking								37
PR & communications								61
Law practice								21
Apparel & fashion								28
Hospitality								13
Government administration								24
Publishing								27
Museums								56
International affairs								46
NGO management								28

Source: Generation i, *The Economist*, September 6, 2014.

journalism and in certain creative fields, unpaid internships have been widespread for decades.

Unpaid internships are so popular now that an industry has developed in which individuals actually pay for the benefit of finding an unpaid experience hoping that it will make them more desirable to employers. Companies like Internship of Your Dreams and Internship .com offer exactly that opportunity. They act like brokers in matching employers, which are often too small to manage campus recruiting, with students for summertime internships. These are especially popular in New York City, where the internship companies may also arrange for housing—all for a fee.[23]

Are these brokered internships worth it? They might very well be, given the importance that employers place on prior work experience, and they do provide an opportunity for students without connections to make them with appropriate firms to get opportunities. They are not unlike the Ivy League summer school classes: Maybe the student couldn't get into Yale, but the fact that he or she did well in a Yale summer program may suggest something about his or her abilities.

Even for unpaid internships, the competition can be ferocious. One college-career counselor told me, "The more elite employers expect candidates for internships to have already had an internship somewhere else"—yet another instance of employers being picky and wanting candidates who can make immediate contributions. And remember, many of these are *unpaid* jobs.

Awareness that unpaid internships in for-profit companies are often illegal is growing, though, in part because of a few well-publicized cases, such as when unpaid interns working on the movie *Black Swan* sued the production company and won in 2013 because the work they did violated the Fair Labor Standards Act.[24] The risk of getting caught is probably pretty low as it takes someone to complain to the government about the unpaid internship, and neither the intern nor the employer is likely to do that. To be fair, though, in many cases employers don't even want those interns because it takes some time and effort to find something useful for them to do, and no one has the time to do that or to train the interns. But often they take them as a favor to their customers or other stakeholders who are trying to find something for their unemployed children to do. The legal attention gives them a reason to say no.

Here's what an unpaid internship requires:

1. The internship, even though it includes actual operation of the facilities of the employer, is similar to training that would be given in an educational environment.
2. The internship experience is for the benefit of the intern.
3. The intern does not displace regular employees but works under close supervision of existing staff.
4. The employer that provides the training derives no immediate advantage from the activities of the intern, and on occasion its operations may actually be impeded.
5. The intern is not necessarily entitled to a job at the conclusion of the internship.
6. The employer and the intern understand that the intern is not entitled to wages for the time spent in the internship.

(continued)

The law that regulates these requirements is the Fair Labor Standards Act. Meeting these conditions can be pretty onerous. It is much easier to do it if the intern is getting college credit for the experience, which is why that arrangement is so popular. For the rules, see U.S. Department of Labor, "Wage and Hour Division (WHD): Fact Sheet #71: Internship Programs Under the Fair Labor Standards Act," April 2010, http://www.dol.gov/whd/regs/compliance/whdfs71.htm.

The *Chronicle of Higher Education* survey asked employers what they would recommend students do who can't get a job in their chosen field. Employers look much more favorably on students with an unpaid internship in the field of their choice than on those who pursue further education in that field. In fact, they prefer volunteer work even in an unrelated field to further education. That suggests that unpaid internships won't go away and that they are a step up from more vocational academic classes.

Despite the fact that internships seem to be more important for getting a job, it is not clear that employers are expanding them. The National Association of College and Employers found a decrease in the number of internships offered between 2013 and 2014 despite the improvement in the economy and despite the fact that two-thirds of interns got offers for full-time jobs (about 80 percent took them).[25]

At the high end, companies are willing to shell out big money to catch those few top students with skills that are in demand right then. The company Glassdoor, which helps match job seekers and employers, reports that the best paid internships, at least among the ones they've examined, are in the software industry in companies like Microsoft, Google, and Amazon, where pay for the summer is equivalent to an annual salary $80,000. These are for the best of the engineering programmers, and the interns are doing real work just like regular employees while they are there.[26]

Even paid internships are not perfect arrangements for learning job skills, of course. A recent survey of college interns found that their expectation that was most often frustrated by their experience was training: They didn't get it often enough or in enough depth.[27]

Alternatives for Work Experience

Employers want evidence that graduates have work skills, and work experience is their preferred measure. What can we do when opportunities to get work experience through internships are limited?

Although no substitute for real work experience, it is possible to provide evidence of some work skills, especially in technical areas, with various kinds of credentials that can be earned relatively cheaply, often through online courses. Among the most popular of these are credentials for software expertise that come with passing standard certification tests. At least some employers are willing to consider them along with academic credentials (see Figure 5.3).

FIGURE 5.3. Consideration of Nontraditional Credentials

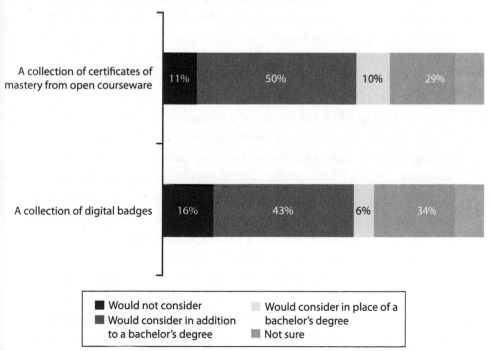

Source: *Chronicle of Higher Education*, 2012.

Digital badges are a credentialing approach in which evidence of skills, however they are learned, is demonstrated through standardized tests. (A good overview of them is offered by the MacArthur Foundation: http://www.macfound.org/programs/digital-badges/.) Certificates of mastery are attached to particular courses. To get a sense of how extensive the world of these certificates is, go to Prometric.com, a company that administers online tests for some of these badges and certificates. Well-known companies like Microsoft and Cisco have large operations that certify the knowledge and skills that individuals have using each company's systems.

Providers of online training like Skilledup.com and Balloon.com aggregate and organize a vast array of online certification courses into a common marketplace easily available to students. Unfortunately, there is no clear or standardized information that allows one to know which certification areas are in demand and which courses are seen as most credible, given that each field is different and that demand changes constantly.

Some certificate programs are quite short, but many require a year or more of classroom-based training. Health care has the most skill certificate programs, accounting for over 40 percent—one reason probably is the many licensing requirements in that field. Keeping track of them has been close to impossible, but a good guess might be that a million or more are issued each year. Figuring out whether these programs are actually a good idea is just as hard a question to answer as whether regular education pays off, and showing that individuals with credentials make more money doesn't answer the question for the same reason that it doesn't for education—the people getting credentials are different from those not getting them, we need to factor in the costs of getting the credentials, and so forth. The results from the few studies that have been done suggest a mixed picture and a great deal of variance in the payoffs associated with different certificates.[28] The fact that the economy is being flooded with credentials no doubt muddies the water by making it harder for employers to know which credentials truly measure skills that are useful at work. In short, while the idea of certifying work-based skills sounds great, so far, it is no panacea.

Enter the Entrepreneurs

By now, the mismatch between students and their families who are desperate to get their kids hired and employers who want candidates with work experience but won't give it to anyone who doesn't already have it probably seems maddening. Colleges are in the middle of that gap, but what they can do in the classroom to address this disconnect is far more limited than their own marketing campaigns suggest.

Maybe it's not a surprise that entrepreneurs smell a market here, and into it they are coming. The most interesting effort to close the work-experience gap has been the rise of programs that promise they can give graduates, for a fee, actual work experience and not just classroom lessons that might be useful in the workplace. Unlike brokers operating in the internship market, these companies provide the work experience themselves.

Businesses like General Assembly put new entrants with no business experience to work on real projects from companies with guidance from experienced hands, teaching practical lessons along the way. Think of these as intense apprenticeship programs. Typically the projects come from nonprofits or start-ups. What "graduates" of the program get, though, is the ability to say that they completed this or that project for the nonprofit and, presumably, a reference from it. DevBootcamp, one of the pioneers in this market, takes graduates with no computer experience and throws them into team-based programming projects for companies, learning lessons about programming as they go. Participants pay for the experience at rates similar to private college tuition—$4,000 for thirty contact hours. Although jobs are not guaranteed at the end, programs like these hint strongly that the organizations providing the projects are interested in hiring the participants after completing the program.

These "boot camps," as they've become known, are becoming so popular that there is actually a company that tracks them—CourseReport.com. It reports on more than 141 businesses that teach skills, mainly computer coding, in this hands-on fashion. It targets what employers say they want, which is demonstrated experience doing real work. In this case, the work is real, although the context isn't.

Of course, the big question is whether these programs actually lead to jobs. A survey of grads across programs finds that 75 percent were in a job after completing the program that required the skills they had just learned. The average completer paid $10,000 in fees, had not worked as a programmer before, and reported a pretty good increase in income after—up 44 percent. Still, 14 percent said that they were unemployed, which is not great, but only 48 percent had full-time jobs before. All this is self-reported data, but that's true for what regular colleges report as well.

An obvious question given the rise of these for-profit programs offering job experience is that if they can make money doing it, why can't regular employers provide similar experiences? There are some good explanations. One might be that companies may not have anyone who can teach the skills that a newbie would need to become, say, a programmer. To take a busy IT professional off his or her job to teach someone else how to do it is expensive, and not everyone is a good teacher. Maybe the biggest reason, at least going forward, is that any company trying to do what these boot camps do would be violating the law. Remember that employers have to pay anyone who is doing work for them that benefits the company. That law is broken all the time, as we saw earlier, but it ought to give employers pause before doing so.

It's probably also true that as these boot camps proliferate, it is only a matter of time before we see reports of big abuses, graduates who can't get jobs and who haven't really learned anything. Remember there is no oversight on these programs the way there is for regular education providers, even the for-profit schools.

What these companies are selling is quite different from what certificates of mastery or digital badges offer. They are essentially getting participants an employer reference, someone who will say that this job candidate did good work building a website for the employer's business. This might not be nearly as valid as what test-based certificates provide, but at least in these fields, employers seem to have confidence in them.

Education providers like Dartmouth's Tuck Business School, Middlebury College, and Berkeley's Haas Business School are also getting into the job skills business. Tuck, for example, has a nonde-gree, no-academic-credit Business Bridge program aimed at recent graduates with no business education or experience. It offers that English major quick, basic business courses and especially counseling and job-seeking help to crack the job market in business. Other pro-grams, like Venture for America, offer training for college grads in how to run start-ups and then puts them to work in those businesses in economically depressed parts of the country.

The idea of paying a company to give you work experience may sound absurd. Is it any worse than paying a college to do the same thing? Let's assume you attend a college that advertises a serious intern-ship program where the college arranges an internship for academic credit during each of the four years of the program. That is the equiva-lent of a semester of internships over the course of the program. If this is a private school where tuition is around $40,000 per year, you will have paid $20,000 for that work experience. Paying a company for some-thing similar seems like a bargain then.

The Temp Marketplace

Temporary help agencies in recent years have become perhaps the most common route into regular employment for students who leave college without full-time jobs. The reason is that temp agencies actu-ally have some ability to build the skill sets of temporary workers and to document those skill sets because they can hire out people at better wages when they do. Many temp agencies offer free training programs—remember that the temps are not regular employees, so the agencies do not have to worry about paying them for any time spent in training. These programs work for the agencies again because they allow them to rent out the temps at higher wages.

The route to regular employment comes from the fact that many employers now use temporary hires as a way to check out workers be-fore they offer full-time jobs to them. If they hire the temp into a full-time job, they typically pay the temp agency a fee, so it works for the agency as well. My research with JR Keller found that about 2 percent of jobs in U.S. companies have been filled by hiring temps into regular jobs.[29] That might not sound like much, but 2 percent of the total number of jobs is more than the number of new graduates entering the labor market in a given year.

There is a view common in some circles that kids today really like to hop from employer to employer, but there is no real evidence for that. In fact, they report a preference for a stable job over higher pay two to one.[30] Younger workers are more able to move because they have fewer constraints tying them down. But that doesn't mean they necessarily want to. Remember, every time someone quits to take a job elsewhere, it is because another employer wanted to hire him or her away.

The Job Market in Summary

A careful look into the way the job market works makes clear that college per se isn't a clear pathway to a good job. In the early days of U.S. education, going to college was a good proxy for who would be successful because only those people from elite backgrounds went to college in the first place. It was a sign of success rather than a cause of success. That changed after World War II when the rise of the great corporations created technical jobs for thousands of engineering graduates and administrative jobs for even more graduates from all kinds of backgrounds. College in those days was a necessary condition to get into the pool of new hires who would then get training for lifetime careers and have their careers mapped out by their companies.

The post–World War II model is fading from view and, with it, that tight connection between college and getting a job. The model we now see has employers wanting to hire applicants who can make contributions immediately, who don't need to be trained. College has attempted to meet that need with a plethora of specific degrees that point directly to jobs. There certainly are many college programs that still translate directly into occupations—or at least first jobs—such as accounting, nursing, education/teaching, engineering, and IT among them. The question is about all the other jobs in the economy.

Employers don't seem all that interested in college educations as providing a firm base on which they can build skills and knowledge. They seem much more interested in job skills.

The problem is that college degrees don't seem to be providing the kind of job skills that employers want. That might not be surprising because the institution of college was set up to provide academic skills, not job skills per se, and the kind of skills that employers want now are very specific to the jobs that need to be performed. Nor is it very efficient for colleges to try to replicate the workplace on their own campus, which is what would be needed to produce those skills.

Internships, co-op programs, and other campus-based connections with employers are great at helping students get jobs. Parents should remember, though, that we are typically paying for those work experiences in the form of tuition because students are doing those work experiences for college credit: Rather than taking a course on world history, they are organizing meetings for a local nonprofit.

Is that a price we are okay with? Maybe not, especially if there are other alternatives. Maybe the appropriate alternative is to let college do what it is good at, which is educating rather than training, focusing on knowledge and life skills rather than job skills, and to find connections into the job market through other paths. Those paths might be low-paid, entry-level jobs, possibly boot camps or practical skills taught elsewhere, or even unpaid internships. That might be a lot better for graduates in the long run because they are learning content in college that will be useful the rest of their lives, not just for a first job. It appears to be better from the perspective of employers doing the hiring than to try to learn practical job skills in school. It also may well make families who would otherwise really struggle to pay for college rethink whether college is necessary for a child that really just wants a job that pays.

6

Conclusions

Is COLLEGE THE key to a good career? It certainly is central to an optimistic view of the future, for young people and for society. Compared to other aspects of life, college is a relatively meritocratic arrangement. Especially in the United States, there are unlimited second chances: Students can drop out, start over, transfer from a community college to a research university, and piece together degrees in all kinds of ways over a long period of time if necessary. Success in college is certainly related to individual effort as well as ability, although it is increasingly possible to push success along by purchasing special help in the form of tutors and support systems. Financial aid based on need provides special support for those who have fewer financial resources. If students do well in studies and other aspects of college life, they can move into professions and get access to lots of things that make up a richer, fuller life.

There is a ton of evidence suggesting that college improves the lives of graduates in many ways. Many of these, such as better health, better citizenship, maturity, and so forth, are also good for society.[1]

In part because of the apparent benefits of college and even more because of the political appeal of offering a merit-based path for individuals to advance, we have expanded the scale of college considerably in the United States. Civic leaders and politicians have promoted the idea that more education and college in particular is the path to advancement. In recent years, though, we have been decidedly less willing to pay for it as taxpayers.

At the same time, the workplace has changed. Good and especially stable jobs with predictable career paths are much more difficult to find. The giant corporations that offered long-term careers have become less significant in the U.S. labor market, fewer companies are interested in hiring individuals with potential and training them to be lifetime employees, and the expectation is that new hires will already have the skills to start contributing. Colleges have moved to persuade students that education can provide those skills.

These trends have come together in ways that are not especially pleasant for the 21 million students currently enrolled in college. The higher-education system has dramatically more students in it than in the past without the equivalent increase in public funding. It has responded by pushing more of the costs onto students and their families. This development is a special burden because the increase in students—up 50 percent since the mid-1990s—is disproportionately from families who are not wealthy, who especially since the Great Recession have struggled with their own job insecurity and ability to pay. For those families, sending kids to college is often a huge financial stretch. At the same time, the ability to stretch financially—and to get into trouble—has gotten easier: Borrowing against your house and against your retirement are common options now that were not available in previous generations.

When those families do stretch, or when individual students have to do it on their own, the burden on them to get a good job at the end is even more urgent. This pressure is driven by another adaptation to higher costs and lower ability to pay, and that is loans, pushing the costs of education onto the graduate's future. Student loans are increasingly used to pay for college, and they can be a crippling burden because interest accumulates at rates well above the level for home mortgages without the ability to ever walk away from them, even through bankruptcy. Both students and their families are often taking on considerable financial risk now to pay for college.

The higher-education system has responded to all this in two important ways. The first is to address that fear about needing a good job, or perhaps more cynically by tapping into it, with new programs that are aimed at getting a job after graduation. The marketing aspects of this response have been led by the new for-profit education providers who almost without exception have targeted students whose primary interest is getting a job after graduation. The second response has been to deliver college degrees in different ways—after hours and off campus—to accommodate students who have to work full-time to pay for college.

These new options change the nature of the college experience in important ways. Eight years of classes for an older adult in an office park after work is not the same thing as four, much more intense years as a young person in residence full-time on a campus where experiences outside of class are designed to help you learn and grow. Yet we often treat them as if they are the same. Even on campus, a job-focused program that mixes course work and internships to teach you how to manage real estate is not going to be the same as a liberal arts program where you learn literature, history, science, and math.

There is no reason to believe that these new options will deliver the same kind of personal and societal benefits that we have attributed to the traditional campus experience, and to be fair, many colleges aren't offering that. The pitch is about getting a good job. It all hangs on that.

Whether these options make sense for students or their families depends crucially on the payoff from them. Will these practical degrees, many of them delivered off campus, really lead to jobs good enough to pay off those student loans or pay back the money parents borrowed against their houses? These are big financial bets for students and their families, and there is a lot of risk in them now. Most people are making those bets on the basis of marketing from colleges and general pronouncements in society that college is necessary for advancement—any good parent should sacrifice to send his or her child there. We can do better than that.

Even if you are not a student or a parent paying for college, these developments in higher education matter a lot because they have a big effect on society. They will alter the nature of the workforce in the future, of citizens and their backgrounds, and of public spending and taxes. College loans, for example, are already the second-biggest source of debt in society, and under- or unemployed grads are a huge drain on families and the social fabric.

We don't know everything about how college is paying off now, certainly not about how it will pay off in the future, but we do know a lot that can make those decisions better. Here's what we know.

The Myths

There are a lot of stories about changes in the workplace that drive wrongheaded ideas about the payoff from a college education. These include the notion that "students today" are doing worse in K–12 school, that the U.S. education system is failing as compared to countries elsewhere, that jobs today and in the future will require more education, that there are lots of good jobs for people if they just had the right education, and that there are shortages of graduates with STEM degrees (science, technology, engineering, and math). There is no support for any of these arguments, and what we do know suggests that they simply aren't true.

The reality is not completely rosy for the U.S. education system, of course. The United States is by far the most expensive college-education system for students and their families. A U.S. family spends about six times as much sending a child to college as does the average family in other developed countries, and we send more students to four-year colleges than any other country does. But we are near the bottom in graduation rates. Although some of our students who have not graduated during traditional college years may eventually get degrees years later, several countries have a higher percentage of college grads than the United States does. Compared to other countries, fewer poor students make it to college here, yet a large proportion of U.S. college students start out taking remedial classes to make up for deficits from high school. The average worker in the United States, indeed in other developed countries as well, already has substantially more education than the jobs they are performing require.

Much has been made of the fact that the average college graduate in the United States makes more than high school grads earn and that the gap between them has been widening. Why that is and what it says for new graduates is not straightforward, however. The gap has increased mainly because of the collapse of wages for those who have less education, not because of any dramatic increase in the earnings of college grads, especially new grads. The reason that fact about the gap matters is because it could well be that college grads do far better than high school grads and still do not earn enough to pay back the cost of their college degrees.

Implicit in the arguments about this college wage premium is the notion that a high school grad would have earned what a college grad earns if only he or she had gone to college. We know that is not true, that kids who go on to college have many advantages over those who do not. Some of those advantages have to do with abilities, some with family background and resources that would have allowed them to do better in life even if they did not go on to college.

Further, what we know from employers is that they seem to value those innate abilities like "leadership" and the ability to demonstrate them in activities outside of class more than they value traditional classroom-based outcomes, which should give us pause about the value of the stripped-down, office-park model of a college education.

The Payoff

The big news about the payoff from college should be the incredible variation in it across colleges. Looking at the actual return on the costs of attending college, careful analyses suggest that the payoff from many college programs—as much as one in four—is actually *negative*. Incredibly, the schools seem to add nothing to the market value of the students. Much of that problem may have to do with the attributes of the students attending those schools, but that should still give us pause about the idea that college pays off for everyone.

For a majority of colleges, the annual return on the investment in attending has been around 7 percent, which may sound great, about what the stock market earns, but the interest rate on unsubsidized student loans is also about 7 percent. There is no guarantee that this rate of return will stay the same in the future. In fact, it appears that the current high level is something of a historical aberration.

The point is that a college degree per se will not necessarily pay off. It depends who you are and where you go.

The Cost Side

The most obvious factors shaping the return are those on the cost side. Although we tend not to think about it often enough, the biggest cost of college comes if a student drops out. It may be awkward socially for a high school grad to wait a year or so before starting college, but sending a student off to college who is not ready for it socially or academically is a bad bet. Chapter 3 outlines what to look for in colleges that reduce their dropout rates. Those programs certainly seem like good things. They also contribute to the high cost of college.

The next most important cost factor is the time it takes to graduate. Given that only 40 percent of full-time students graduate on time and only 60 percent make it out in six years, the time it takes to finish a degree varies a lot and adds to costs dramatically. The probability of taking longer than four years to graduate—indeed the risk of dropping out—are rarely included in calculations of the rate of return. These are also factors over which colleges have a great deal of control, in part again through support programs. A more expensive private school with all these support programs that graduates virtually all of its freshmen in four years may actually be cheaper overall than a state university where freshmen take more years to finish.

The most controllable factor delaying graduation is the difficulty in completing the requirements of majors on time. Complicated majors with lots of requirements, especially advanced courses that have many prerequisites that have to be taken in a particular order, can break down in many ways and delay graduation. These delays are especially likely if students switch majors, something that may be necessary to get a good return.

It is next to impossible to figure out what the true cost of college will be until one applies and receives an answer about possible financial aid that the school might offer. Figuring out the nuances of financial aid has created its own industry, but the benefits of trying to game the system in any significant way—switching assets around to increase eligibility—create legal issues and frankly don't seem worth doing. The basic lesson about aid is that the downsides of applying for it are trivial and the upside can be substantial. It is worth paying for help to figure out the applications if that is a hurdle.

Having information on any financial aid package leads to two important judgment calls. The first concerns merit-based aid, where a college is willing to discount the price to attract students who would otherwise not attend. Sometimes merit aid is designed to attract more students from particular parts of the United States, sometimes it is targeted to attract students with unusual backgrounds, and most often it is used to get students whose academic record is better than the average of other students attending the college. Is it worth essentially trading down to attend a less selective school to cut the costs? It may well be, at least in terms of the financial payoff from the degree. As we discuss in Chapter 4, the evidence that graduates of elite schools do better in the job market simply because they went to an elite school is not strong.

The second judgment call concerns the amount of loans that make up a financial aid package. We have probably not taken these loans seriously enough in the past. Unless a graduate gets a pretty good job right out of college, student loans can be crippling financially. Using loans to pay for a degree that may not have an immediate payoff is a huge and probably bad risk. Trading down to attend a less prestigious school that offers more merit aid to reduce the amount of loans may be a very smart financial decision.

The Benefit Side

The hardest part of the financial equation to calculate is the job side: What kind of job awaits the graduate? The quality of those jobs depends on supply and demand, something that is constantly in a state of flux. The fact that so many of the hot fields in a particular year are in technology-related fields has contributed to perhaps the biggest myth about the college job market, the idea that those jobs are always hot. The complaint that follows is that students somehow just aren't pursuing the right majors and that they could get good jobs if only they'd pick those obvious, technical fields.

In fact, science and math jobs have never been particularly hot, and the subfields within engineering and technology jobs blow hot and cold. As described in Chapter 4, petroleum engineering, a field that was in deep slumber a decade ago, is the hottest job in the United States right now. The reason is because of supply and demand, precisely because we could not anticipate the fracking boom that generated so much demand for these skills. Just before this boom, the job market for these skills was dead. Few students chose to major in it, so the supply was down. Demand then jumped up with fracking, leading to a supply-demand imbalance and high wages for the small group of new petroleum engineers. Engineering is a boom-and-bust field. The fact that the specializations within engineering are not substitutes for each other—aeronautical engineers can't do petroleum engineering jobs—means that one field could be way up while another is way down, which is often the case. Much the same thing happened with IT careers, which have gone through their own boom-and-bust cycles and where one specialty can be red hot while another is cold.

The fact that students are chasing these hot careers actually makes them more risky because the students' response creates more variability: Students who poured into the IT job market during the 1990s boom, for example, graduated just about the time demand faded, after the Y2K experience and the 2001 recession. All that extra supply of IT talent pushed wages and job prospects down even further. That, in turn, discouraged students from pursuing the IT field, exacerbating the shortfall of supply when demand for IT began to recover after the Great Recession.

In short, the jobs that get the attention in any year for being the place to be get that way precisely because we didn't know, probably couldn't know, that they would be the place to be.

If you are a student, you need to go into these high-risk labor markets with your eyes open because they imply high risk for the payoff from a college degree. What we can do to reduce the risk is reserve the ability to switch majors until the last minute. Settling on a field a year before graduating allows us to time the changing job market much better than picking a field when you apply to college five years before (assuming you actually get out in four years). That advice helps us see why the ability to switch majors and complete them on time is so important in choosing colleges.

Figuring out what the job prospects are like for a degree program at a particular college is tricky because often the colleges don't know themselves. How their graduates are doing is something they can only learn by finding where they are—harder to do than you might think—and then asking them to tell. The response rates to these surveys are miserable, and there is a strong sense that the grads doing poorly don't reply and also that many people make up the answers. Many colleges spin the information they have to make their performance look better, such as counting a graduate with any kind of job, even temp work, as "employed," excluding those who say they have given up looking, and so forth. In short, don't count on the college for accurate evidence.

It helps to do your own market research by seeing what the overall job market in the United States is like in whatever field is of interest. Sites like the National Association of Colleges and Employers provide some of that information for recent grads. The most important research you can do is to visit a college's career center for yourself to see which employers come to recruit there and what jobs they are trying to fill.

Knowing what the market is like today doesn't tell you much about where it will be in the future, of course. It is important to think through what you will have gotten out of your degree if the market for it is not so hot when you graduate. The opportunities are more limited the more focused the program is: If the pharma industry is down, where else can you use that pharmaceutical marketing degree? If you change your mind once you are in the program—a very large percentage of students do—how easy is it to switch to something different?

Maybe most important, ask what you are learning in a program that will be useful after you get that first job. College should be preparation for a lifetime. First jobs don't last very long, and it is common now for employees to find that they have to reinvent themselves for different jobs. If that degree isn't much good after you get your first job because the knowledge you learned isn't useful elsewhere and also goes out of date quickly, that degree is pretty risky and not so valuable.

Putting all these caveats together may put a damper on the attractiveness of a degree designed to teach occupational skills that get you the first job, especially once we realize that employers don't seem to care that much about job skills learned in college.

Certainly there are exceptions in long-standing fields like accounting and nursing where degrees may be required by regulations and industry standards, but what actual employers say about college job candidates upends the conventional wisdom: Work experience is more important that classroom lessons, and experiences associated with the Ivory Tower residential experience—running clubs, being on athletic teams—seem to be at least as important as the classroom. The academic skills employers say they want, such as better decision making and communications skills, are ones we associate with traditional college programs including liberal arts, not applied, job-focused knowledge and skills.

That insight opens the door to alternative paths to the first job. It is not necessary to have a degree in retail management to work for a big department-store chain. A major in any field, a good record of college experiences, summer jobs in retail that lead to good references, and some practical courses taken anywhere might be more than enough. A fine arts major with a couple of programming classes taken in the last year of college and some volunteer experience doing programming work is more than sufficient for many programming jobs, and then you can still have the education in fine arts that your heart desired. Even paying to get job experience if necessary is reasonable when compared to the alternative of paying a college to get it for you.

Policy Implications

Policy discussions about higher education in the United States have pushed the idea that because college degrees pay off for individuals, it is reasonable to make students pay for them, if not up front then later on with loans. As we have seen, though, the assertion that college necessarily pays off is not true, and paying for it yourself especially with loans can be a crippling decision financially. At the very least, we should be less blithe about encouraging students to go for that degree and much more circumspect about the risks of doing so. The risks can be understood and managed, but it takes real effort to do that.

A college education is a huge financial decision for many families, and the rhetoric that college is the only path to a good job will push many of them off a financial cliff. It is one thing to push students to take advantage of a free education; it's another to suggest that they go into debt to do it because it will pay off. We wouldn't be allowed to give that kind of financial advice if we were in the investment business, and we shouldn't give it here.

The policy world should begin by recognizing basic facts about labor markets. The first is that we can't predict where the economy will be and which jobs will be in demand years into the future. Employers who say that we need more engineers or IT grads are not promising to hire them when they graduate in four years. Pushing kids into a field like health care because someone believes there is a need there now will not guarantee that they all get jobs and, if they do, that those jobs will be as good as workers in that field have now. In fact, if we really move a lot of students in that direction, say, by pushing up funding for those programs and cutting it in other areas, as some people have suggested, we will increase the supply of candidates and, absent a boom in demand, cause wages to fall and many health care grads to struggle finding a job. We will cause the problem we are trying to solve.

A second fact about labor markets is that they create winners and losers, especially in the tension between employers and employees, buyers and sellers. Yes, it helps employers in any industry to have a big supply of very bright, hardworking applicants, but it is better for the applicants to be in a market where the supply is scarce relative to demand. One could make a strong argument that the steady supply of graduates in fields like engineering, subsidized by large engineering programs in most state universities, actually made it easier for employers to churn through engineering employees because they can return to campuses to hire new ones with new skills. It might be one thing to argue that it is in the national interest for an industry like IT to get really sharp and high-paid minds to invent the next generation of technology. It is another to say that we need a steady supply of low-wage programmers.

We shouldn't pretend that what works for employers necessarily works for job applicants. It would be a tricky business for governments—state and local in particular—to see themselves through their local colleges as the supplier of labor to employers and then to have to explain to parents why the degree that their college pushed students to pursue did not lead to a good job four years later. The reasons why governments are—and should be—reluctant to pick winners and losers in industries ought to apply to labor markets as well. If we have been willing to tolerate unemployment and underemployment among recent grads, we might also want to tolerate tighter labor markets that cause their wages to go up.

The evidence from employers that what they want from recent graduates is less about classroom knowledge and more about experiences outside the classroom works against another popular policy argument, that we should offer cut-rate, low-cost college degrees in order to provide more of them to more students. So far at least, it does not appear that employers will want students with those degrees.

Where the policy world could do important work is in improving the information that applicants have about the quality of different education providers. State governments have been active at prosecuting outright fraud in the claims and operations of for-profit colleges, but the problem is much broader than that. It is the absence of valid information of almost any kind to use in assessing whether particular degrees will pay off.

A final conundrum for policy—and it is a big one—is what to do about the fact that employers seem much less willing to provide training for new graduates and are asking state and local governments to pay for it. A recent example of this is the new shipyard in Mobile, Alabama, where the state heavily subsidized the training of 3,000 workers as part of an aid package to attract a shipbuilding company to Mobile. Admittedly this issue is more about skills associated with associate degrees, but it spills over to bachelor's grads as well, especially in those technical fields. New grads often find themselves in a real Catch-22 with respect to work skills: Employers only want to hire applicants who already have skills, but no one wants to give the new grads the opportunity to learn those skills on the job.

Clearly there is a small-government objection to having taxpayers fund something like training that employers usually pay for themselves, but there are already many subsidies of other kinds from state and local governments to attract and keep businesses. That ship sailed a while ago. It is probably better to use government funds for training and education than for outright subsidies. The same applies for college education. Given that subsidies to employers are going to happen anyway, it is hard to argue with state and local governments paying for education that aids particular employers. The bright line, though, is when the government tries to get applicants or employees to pay for that education. That pushes risk onto the students and does so in ways they are unlikely to understand.

We can understand why politicians don't want to say it, but unfortunately, education is just not a panacea for the difficulties that individuals now face in the job market. It is certainly true that college has been life changing for most people and a tremendous financial investment for many of them. It is also true that for some people, it has been financially crippling. To make an obvious point, not all college experiences are the same, and not all students are the same. At least from the financial perspective, not all degrees are going to pay off financially, and not all students are going to be able to earn a return on their investment in college.

The world of college education is different now than it was a generation ago, when many of the people driving policy decisions on education went to college, and the theoretical ideas about why college should pay off do not comport well with the reality. Among other things, we now have an education industry with a financial interest in getting kids into schools by marketing the idea that there are big financial benefits to going to college. Suggesting that everyone should go to college without thinking through how they are going to pay for it is reckless. Consumer protection for students and their families is worth considering, and the information provided here is a start in that direction.

Appendix

FIGURE A.1. Course Taking by High School Students: Average Number of Credits Earned in Each Subject Area by Public High School Graduates, 1990 to 2009

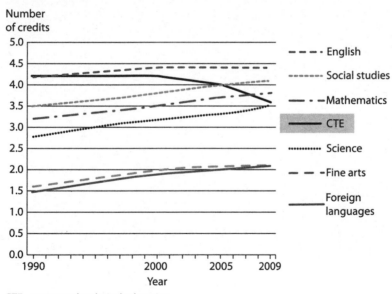

CTE=career and technical education
Source: NCES Career/Technical Education Statistics.

FIGURE A.2. Desirability of Nontraditional Bachelor's Degrees Versus Traditional Four-Year Degree

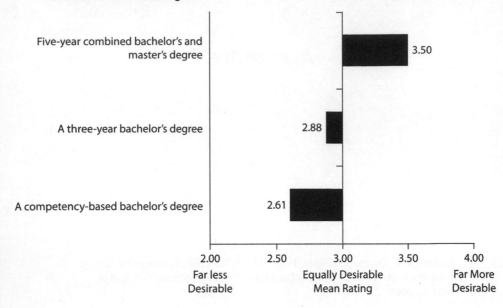

FIGURE A.3. Average 2013–2014 In-State Tuition and Fees at Public Four-Year and Two-Year Institutions, by State, and Five-Year Percentage Changes in Inflation-Adjusted Tuition and Fees, 2008–1009 to 2013–2014

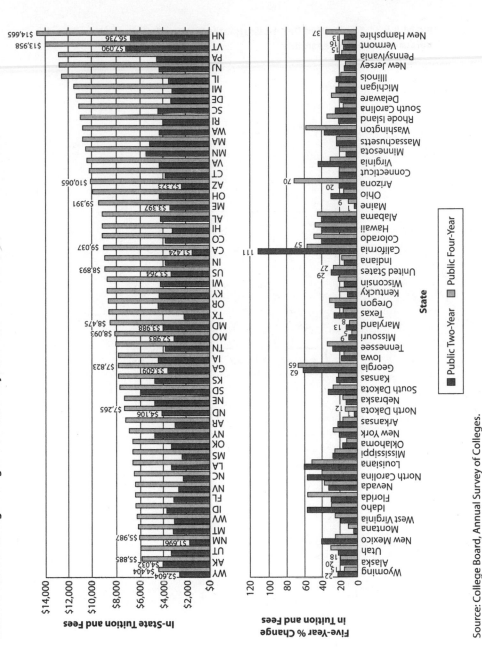

Source: College Board, Annual Survey of Colleges.

FIGURE A.4. Top Skills of Recent Graduates Seeking Positions: Have, Need, Versus College Responsibility

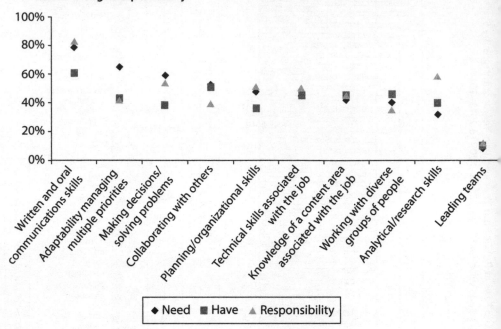

◆ Need   ■ Have   ▲ Responsibility

Notes

1. Why Do People with More Education Get Better Jobs?

1. Joseph Arum and Josipa Rocksa, *Aspiring Adults Adrift: Tentative Transitions of College Graduates* (Chicago: University of Chicago Press, 2014).

2. These results come from a survey of recent school leavers: Board of Governors of the Federal Reserve System, *In the Shadow of the Great Recession: Experiences and Perspectives of Young Workers* (November 2014).

3. See Mandi Woodruff, "7 College Graduates Whose Lives Were Wrecked by Student Loan Debt," *Business Insider*, June 6, 2013, http://www.business-insider.com/students-loan-debt-horror-stories-2013-6?op=1.

4. "Shorts and Faces: Ivory Hunting on the Charles," *Fortune* 37 (January 1948): 116.

5. For more on the breakdown of training and long-term careers, see Peter Cappelli, *The New Deal at Work: Managing the Market-Driven Workforce* (Boston: Harvard Business School Press, 1999).

6. See Steven F. Hipple and Emy Sok, "Tenure of American Workers," *Spotlight on Statistics*, U.S. Bureau of Labor Statistics, 2013, http://www.bls.gov/spotlight/2013/tenure/pdf/tenure.pdf; and Matthew Bidwell, "What Happened to Long-Term Employment? The Role of Worker Power and Environmental Turbulence in Explaining Declines in Worker Tenure," *Organization Science*, 24, no. 4 (2013): 1061–1082.

7. See Lisa M. Lynch and Sandra E. Black, "Beyond the Incidence of Employer Provided Training," Industrial and Labor Relations Review 52, no. 1 (1998): 64–81 for these results, and Harley J. Frazis, Diane E. Herz, and Michael W. Horrigan, "Employer Provided Training: Results from a New Survey," *Monthly Labor Review* 118, no. 5 (1995): 3–17 for other evidence on the extent of training.

8. References for these data are in Peter Cappelli, "Skill Shortages, Skill Gaps, and Skill Mismatches: Evidence and Arguments for the U.S.," *ILR Review*, April 2015.

9. National Center for Education Statistics (NCES), *The Condition of Education*, tables 20 and 233; and NCES, *Digest of Educational Statistics*, table 302.30.

10. Rodney Andrews, Jing Li, and Michael F. Lovenheim, "Heterogeneous Paths Through College: Detailed Patterns and Relationships with Graduation and Earnings" (NBER Working Paper No. 19935, February 2014, JEL No. I21, I23, J31).

11. NCES, "Fast Facts: Graduation Rates," n.d., http://nces.ed.gov/fastfacts /display.asp?id=40 (accessed September 2014).

12. See Board of Governors of the Federal Reserve System, *In the Shadow of the Great Recession*.

13. NCES, Characteristics of Postsecondary Students, May 2014, http://nces .ed.gov/programs/coe/indicator_csb.asp.

14. Robert Zemsky, *Checklist for Change: Making American Higher Education a Sustainable Enterprise* (New Brunswick, NJ: Rutgers University Press, 2013).

15. John Bound, Michael Lovenheim, and Sarah Turner, "Why Have College Completion Rates Declined? An Analysis of Changing Student Preparation and Collegiate Resources" (NBER Working Paper No. 15566, December 2009).

16. See Institute of Education Sciences, National Center for Education Statistics, "First-Year Undergraduate Remedial Coursetaking: 1999–2000, 2003–04, 2007–08," *Statistics in Brief*, January 2013. Sixteen percent of four-year students in private colleges took remedial courses in 2000, versus 15 percent in 2008, almost no change.

17. NCES, *Digest of Educational Statistics*, tables 305.30 and 305.40 for 2012–2013.

18. See Kevin Carey, "For Accomplished Students, Reaching a Good College Isn't as Hard as It Seems," *New York Times*, November 29, 2014.

19. Caroline M. Hoxby, "The Changing Selectivity of American Colleges" (NBER Working Paper No. 15446, October 2009).

20. College Board, *Trends in College Pricing*, 2013.

21. Annalisa Merelli, "It's Harder to Get a Job in Italy with a College Degree Than Without One," Quartz, November 8, 2013, http://qz.com /145217/its-harder-to-get-a-job-in-italy-with-a-college-degree-than-with outone/.

22. James A. Freeman and Barry T. Hirsch, "College Majors and the Knowledge Content of Jobs," *Economics of Education Review* 27 (2007): 517–535.

23. Peter Arcidiacono, V. Joseph Hotz, and Songman Kang, "Modeling College Major Choices Using Elicited Measures of Expectations and Counterfactuals" (NBER Working Paper No. 15729, 2010).

24. Ron Wolff, "Too Many Students Pursue Worthless Degrees," *News Herald*, December 1, 2012.

25. See John Siegfried and Malcolm Getz, "Where Do the Children of Professors Attend College?," *Economics of Education Review* 25, no. 2 (2006): 201–210.

26. "When Tuition at CUNY Was Free, Sort Of," *CUNY Newswire*, October 12, 2011, http://www1.cuny.edu/mu/forum/2011/10/12/when-tuition-at -cuny-was-free-sort-of/.

27. Rob Kuznia, "Special Guest Bill Clinton Delivers Redondo Union High Commencement Speech," *Daily Breeze*, June 14, 2012, http://www.dailybreeze .com/general-news/20120615/special-guest-bill-clinton-delivers-redondo-union -high-commencement-speech.

28. For an account, see Loren Steffy, "Could Oil-Fed Enrollment Boom Lead to Bust at US Colleges?," *Forbes*, June 25, 2013, http://www.forbes.com/sites /lorensteffy/2013/06/25/could-oil-fed-enrollment-boom-lead-to-bust-at-u-s -colleges/.

29. http://www.high-school.devry.edu/parents.jsp.

30. For DeVry's statistics, see DeVry University, "DeVry University Graduate Employment Statistics," 2013, http://www.devry.edu/d/us-combined-graduates -employment-statistics.pdf.

31. Unpublished data from National Association of Colleges and Employers.

32. Kuznia, "Special Guest Bill Clinton." The lower unemployment rate for college grads has not always been the case, and it appears to be so because when there are not enough jobs around for the college grads, they take jobs that high school grads would otherwise do. There is no evidence that the lower unemployment rate for college grads means that there are more jobs that require college-level skills, which is typically the implication drawn from that data.

33. For more on GED certificates, see David Boesel, Nabeel Alsalam, and Thomas M. Smith, *Educational and Labor Market Performance of GED Recipients* (Washington, DC: U.S. Department of Education, Office of Educational Research and Improvement, National Library of Education, 1998).

34. See Phillip L. Roth, Craig A. BeVier, Fred S. Switzer III, and Jeffery S. Schippman, "Meta-Analyzing the Relations Between Grades and Job Performance," *Journal of Applied Psychology* 81, no. 5 (1996): 548–556.

35. The amount of variance explained by a correlation is obtained by squaring its value. Hence, a correlation of 0.16 (r = .16) implies an $R^2 = 0.025$. For

evidence that performance in college classrooms does mimic some aspects of job requirements, see Peter Cappelli, "Rethinking the 'Skills Gap,'" *California Management Review* 37, no. 4 (1995): 108–124. For a review of the studies on grades and job performance, see Roth et al., "Meta-Analyzing the Relationship." Google's experience is described in Adam Bryant, "In Head-Hunting, Big Data May Not Be Such a Big Deal," *New York Times,* June 19, 2013.

36. Yukon Huang and Canyon Bosler, "China's Burgeoning Graduates—Too Much of a Good Thing?," *National Interest,* January 7, 2014, http://nationalinterest .org/commentary/china%E2%80%99s-burgeoning-graduates%E2%80%94 too-much-good-thing-9674.

37. Richard B. Freeman, "A Cobweb Model of the Supply and Starting Salaries of New Engineers," *Industrial and Labor Relations Review* 29, no. 2 (1976): 236–248.

38. For more detail on the recent labor market for college grads in China, see Bob Davis, "Graduates Play It Safe and Lose Out," *Wall Street Journal,* March 25, 2013, http://online.wsj.com/news/articles/SB1000142412788732467860457833 40530200654140; and Shawn Mahoney, "Graduate Unemployment in China and the US," *China Daily Mail,* August 17, 2012, http://chinadailymail.com/2012/08 /17/graduate-unemployment/.

39. See Bureau of Labor Statistics, table 1.4, http://www.bls.gov/emp/ep _table_104.htm.

40. The scholarship from the Klingon Language Institute and others like it can be found at Melissa Tamura, "45 of the Weirdest College Scholarships," CollegeXpress, http://www.collegexpress.com/lists/list/45-of-the-weirdest -college-scholarships/1000/ (accessed September 2014).

2. How Are We Doing?

1. The National Commission on Excellence in Education, *A Nation at Risk: The Imperative for Educational Reform* (Washington, DC: U.S. Department of Education, 1983).

2. National Center for Education Statistics, "Status Dropout Rates," The Condition of Education, last updated January 2014, http://nces.ed.gov/programs /coe/indicator_coj.asp.

3. For the most recent comparative data on student achievement, see the Programme on International Student Achievement, http://www.oecd.org/pisa /keyfindings/pisa-2012-results.htm. For the evidence on early rankings, see Tom Loveless, *2011 Brown Center Report on American Education: How Well Are American Students Learning?,* vol. III, no. 1, Brown Center on Educational Policy (Washington, DC: The Brookings Institute, 2012). For evidence on cram schools, see Mark Bray and Chad Lykins, *Shadow Education: Private Supplementary*

Tutoring and Its Implications for Policy Makers in Asia (Mandaluyong City, Philippines: Asian Development Bank, 2012).

4. See National Center for Educational Statistics, Digest of Educational Statistics, U.S. Department of Education, tables 312 and 313.

5. See OECD, *Education at a Glance* (Paris: OECD, 2013); chart A4.1 reports comparative graduation rates, B1.2 presents comparative spending data, and A1.1 contains family expenditures. The United States is one of the few countries where the younger cohort, age twenty-five to thirty-four, does not have more education than older workers do, true also for Israel, Finland, Germany, and Brazil. The shortfall in the U.S. cohort is attributable only to men. The younger cohort in the United States is far more likely to earn college degrees later in life than are those in other countries, though, so the U.S. position in the rankings should change. Whether and how the U.S. position in rankings like these matters is not obvious, though.

6. The private spending on postsecondary education also includes any donations to private colleges. For more on the relative position of the United States, see OECD, *Country Note: Education at a Glance—US 2012* (Paris: OECD), http://www.oecd.org/education/CN%20-%20United%20States.pdf.

7. For a review of these developments, see H. Gordon, *The History and Growth of Vocational Education in America*, 2nd ed. (Prospect Heights, IL: Waveland, 2003).

8. BLS, table 2.17. Here NCES data suggests slightly different trends using different occupational classifications (CTE, figure 2). The percentage of students earning credits in the "construction" area fell only slightly from 1990 to 2009, by 0.7 percent. The percentage in "manufacturing," which would include machinist skills, fell by 9.5 percent. Interestingly, "business" coursework declined by almost 20 percent, while at the undergraduate level, it expanded considerably in the same period. These data only say whether students are taking any courses, in contrast to the BLS data, which indicate how many courses they are taking (see CTE, table h125).

9. Curiously, the number of "program completers" remains unchanged over this period, at just over 50,000, even though the number of programs and the number of apprentices declined sharply. That translates to about two completers per apprentice program each year. See U.S. Department of Labor Employment and Training Administration, Registered Apprenticeship National Results, http://www.doleta.gov/oa/data_statistics.cfm.

10. See María Prada and Sergio Urzúa, "One Size Does Not Fit All: Multiple Dimensions of Ability, College Attendance, and Wages" (NBER Working Paper 20752, 2014).

11. See National Center on Education and Statistics, U.S. Department of Education, table 302.60.

12. W. Norton Grubb and Marvin Lazerson, *The Education Gospel: The Economic Power of Schooling* (Cambridge, MA: Harvard University Press, 2004).

13. See, e.g., David J. Deming, Claudia Goldin, and Lawrence F. Katz, "The For-Profit Postsecondary School Sector: Nimble Critters or Agile Predators?" (NBER Working Paper 17710, 2011); and Anna S. Chung, "Choice of For-Profit College," *Economics of Education Review* 31, no. 6 (2012): 1084–1101.

14. For the Indian story, see Andre Beteille, *Universities at the Crossroads* (Oxford: Oxford University Press, 2010). For the situation in Italy, see ANSA, "Students March Against Renzi Reforms," October 10, 2014, http://www.ansa.it. For the U.S. version, see Michael Roth, "How to Destroy College Education," *New York Times*, June 23, 2014.

15. Melissa Korn, "Party Ends at For-Profit Colleges," *Wall Street Journal*, August 23, 2011.

16. Last Week Tonight with John Oliver, "Student Debt (HBO)," YouTube, September 7, 2014, http://www.youtube.com/watch?v=P8pjd1QEA0c.

17. Morgan Cloud and George B. Shepherd, "Law Deans in Jail" (Research Paper No. 12-199, Emory University School of Law Legal Studies Research Paper Series, 2014).

18. This list comes from ACT, *What Works in Student Retention: Fourth National Survey: Report for All Colleges and Universities*, 2010, http://www.act.org /research/policymakers/pdf/droptables/AllInstitutions.pdf.

19. For details, see Goldie Blumenstyk, "Blowing Off Class? We Know," *New York Times*, December 2, 2014.

20. The list is derived from Veronica A. Lotkowski, Steven B. Robbins, and Richard J. North, *The Role of Academic and Non-Academic Factors in Improving College Retention*, ACT Policy Report, 2004, http://www.act.org/research /policymakers/pdf/college_retention.pdf.

21. Philip Babcock and Mindy Marks, "The Falling Time Cost of College: Evidence from Half a Century of Time Use Data," *Review of Economics and Statistics* 93, no. 2 (2011): 468–478.

22. Bruce Sacerdote, "Peer Effects with Random Assignment: Results for Dartmouth Roommates," *Quarterly Journal of Economics* 116, no. 2 (2001): 681–704.

23. Todd Stinebrickner and Ralph Stinebrickner, "Learning About Academic Ability and the College Dropout Decision," *Journal of Labor Economics* 30, no. 4 (2012): 707–748; Ralph Stinebrickner and Todd R. Stinebrickner, "A Major in Science? Initial Beliefs and Final Outcomes for College Major and Dropout," *Review of Economic Studies* 81, no. 1 (2014): 426–472.

24. See, e.g., Marissa Hartwig and John Dunlosky, "Study Strategies of College Students: Are Self-Testing and Scheduling Related to Achievement?," *Psychonomic Bulletin & Review* 19, no. 1 (2012): 126–134.

25. Wharton School, University of Pennsylvania, "Undergrad Program: PennSTART," 2009, https://spike.wharton.upenn.edu/ugrprogram/transfers/pennstart.cfm.

26. Edith Wagner and Ştefan Szamosközi, "Effects of Direct Academic Motivation Enhancing Intervention Programs: A Meta-Analysis," *Journal of Cognitive & Behavioral Psychotherapies* 12, no. 1 (2012): 85–98; Harvard University, Success-Failure Project, http://successfailureproject.bsc.harvard.edu/.

27. Stanford University, Resilience Project, https://undergrad.stanford.edu/resilience.

28. The program actually requires that participants already be the equivalent of a junior in college, so only the last two years of the bachelor's degree will be an online experience.

3. Does College Pay Off?

1. Daron Acemoglu and David Autor, "What Does Human Capital Do? A Review of Goldin and Katz's *The Race Between Education and Technology*" (NBER Working Paper No. 17820, February 2012), figure 3.

2. David Leonard, "Is College Worth It? Clearly, New Data Say," *New York Times*, May 27, 2014. Estimates by the *New York Times* put the hourly college wage premium higher, up to 98 percent in 2013.

3. Robert E. Hall, "Quantifying the Lasting Harm to the U.S. Economy from the Financial Crisis" (NBER Working Paper No. 20183, May 2014).

4. Paul Beaudry, David A. Green, and Benjamin M. Sand, "The Great Reversal in the Demand for Skill and Cognitive Tasks" (NBER Working Paper 18901, 2013), 3. An earlier argument suggests that the trend for college-educated men to end up in jobs that require less than a college degree started earlier. David Autor, "The Polarization of Job Opportunities in the U.S. Labor Market: Implications for Employment and Earnings" (Washington, DC: Center for American Progress and the Hamilton Project, 2010).

5. It is also true that, over time, students with less innate ability and advantages were more likely to attend four-year colleges. That would depress the average outcomes for college grads, except for the fact that many of those additional lower-ability students do not graduate from college. They would fall into the "some college" category. Their wages are much lower than those for college grads, and the gap has grown over time. The college premium I report here is lower than the ones typically reported in the press because of that GED category: These results come from data by the National Center on Educational Statistics, whose high school graduate measure does not include GED holders; the stories in the press rely on data from the Current Population Survey, in which GED holders are included with high school graduates.

6. See Heidi Shierholz, Alyssa Davis, and Will Kimballm, "The Class of 2014: The Weak Economy Is Idling Too Many Young Graduates" (EPI Briefing Paper 377, 2014).

7. For a review of this work, see E. Leuven and H. Oosterbeek, "Overeducation and Mismatch in the Labor Market," in *Handbook of the Economics of Education*, vol. 4, ed. E. Hanushek, S. Machin, and L. Woessmann (Waltham, MA: Elsevier, 2011). For recent evidence on the United States, see Brian Clark, Clément Joubert, and Arnaud Maurel, "The Career Prospects of Overeducated Americans" (NBER Working Paper 20167, May 2014), http://www.nber.org/papers/w20167.

8. John Schmitt and Heather Boushey, *The College Conundrum: Why the Benefits of a College Education May Not Be So Clear, Especially to Men* (Washington, DC: Center for American Progress, December 2010).

9. For a review, see Jessica Bennett and Seamus McGuinness, "Assessing the Impact of Skill Shortages on the Productivity Performance of High-Tech Firms in Northern Ireland," *Applied Economics* 41, no. 6 (2009): 727–737. Stephan Kampelmann and François Rycx, *The Impact of Educational Mismatch on Firm Productivity: Evidence from Linked Panel Data, Economics of Education Review* 31, no. 6 (2012): 918–931, show positive productivity effects associated with overeducated workforces in Belgium.

10. Among the recent studies showing this effect are Yuji Genda, Ayako Kondo, and Souichi Ohta, "Long-Term Effects of a Recession at Labor Market Entry in Japan and the United States," *Journal of Human Resources* 45 (2010): 157–196; Lisa B. Kahn, "The Long-Term Labor Market Consequences of Graduating from College in a Bad Economy," *Labour Economics* 17 (2010): 303–316; and Philip Oreopoulos, Till von Wachter, and Andrew Heisz, "The Short- and Long-Term Career Effects of Graduating in a Recession," *American Economic Journal: Applied Economics* 4, no. 1 (2012): 1–29.

11. Michael Greenstone and Adam Looney, "Where Is the Best Place to Invest $102,000—in Stocks, Bonds, or a College Degree?," Hamilton Project, June 25, 2011, http://www.hamiltonproject.org/files/downloads_and_links/06_college_value.pdf.

12. See PayScale, "2014 Payscale College ROI Report," http://www.payscale.com/college-roi/full-list/sortby/AnnualRoi/financial-aid/yes (accessed October 2014).

13. See Louis Lavelle, "College ROI: What We Found," *Businessweek*, April 9, 2012, http://www.businessweek.com/articles/2012-04-09/college-roi-what-we-found#p2.

14. Peter Cappelli, Monika Hamori, and Rocio Bonet, "Whose Got Those Top Jobs?," *Harvard Business Review* (2014).

15. Caroline Hoxby, "The Return from Graduating from an Elite School, 1960 to 1988," in *Forum Futures: Exploring the Future of Higher Education, 2000*

Papers, ed. Maureen Devlin and Joel Meyerson, 13–42 (San Francisco: Jossey-Bass, 2001).

16. CollegeMeasures.org, *Higher Education Pays: But a Lot More for Some Graduates Than for Others* (Washington, DC: CollegeMeasures.org, 2014).

17. Stacey Dale and Alan B. Krueger, "Estimating the Payoff to Attending a More Selective College: An Application of Selection on Observables and Unobservables," *Quarterly Journal of Economics* 117, no. 4 (2002): 1491–1527; Stacey Dale and Alan B. Krueger, "Estimating the Return to College Selectivity over the Career Using Administrative Earnings Data" (NBER Working Paper No. 17159, 2011).

18. Mark Hoekstra, "The Effect of Attending the Flagship State University on Earnings: A Discontinuity-Based Approach," *Review of Economics and Statistics* 91, no. 4 (2009): 717–724.

19. Kevin Lang and Erez Siniver, "Why Is an Elite Undergraduate Education Valuable? Evidence from Israel" (NBER Working Paper No. 16730, 2011).

20. For evidence on the relationship between firm-based screening and the returns on education, see Sarah Brown and John G. Sessions, "Evidence on the Relationship between Firm-Based Screening and the Returns to Education," *Economics of Education Review* 25, no. 5 (2006): 498–509.

21. Rodney J. Andrews, Jing Li, and Michael F. Lovenheim, "Quantile Treatment Effects of College Quality on Earnings: Evidence from Administrative Data in Texas" (NBER Working Paper No. 18068, 2012).

4. The Cost of Going to College

1. Comparative data on college costs is contained in OECD, *Education at a Glance* (Paris: OECD, 2013); table B1.1, while data on family payments is in, table A7.3.

2. See University of Pennsylvania, Archives and Records Center, "University History: Tuition and Mandated Fees, Room and Board and Other Educations Costs at Penn," http://www.archives.upenn.edu/histy/features/tuition/main.html.

3. The Educational Opportunity Grants program created need-based grants for low-income students that did not need to be repaid, and the 1964 Educational Opportunity Act created work-study programs by giving schools funds for employing low-income students in jobs on campus. A series of new laws helped cement the need-based aspect of financial aid: The 1965 Higher Education Act provided federal-government-backed insurance for privately issued, need-based student loans, created rules governing those loans, and added more need-based grants for undergrads (this program became known as Pell Grants in 1972). Legislation in the 1980s sought to ensure that financial aid was targeted only to people in financial need, and the Higher Education Amendments of 1992

mandated the use of a common formula for determining need and the associated aid, eliminating the use of the CSS application. Some private schools continued to use a modified version of the CSS application to award their own, nongovernmental aid, which was still need based. A number of sources describe the key legislative developments and practices in U.S. financial aid, such as "History of Student Financial Aid," http://www.finaid.org/educators/history.phtml (accessed October 2014), while developments at the state and local level are reviewed in R. Chen and E. P. St. John, "State Financial Policies and College Student Persistence: A National Study," *The Journal of Higher Education*, 82, no. 5 (2011): 629–660.

4. For a discussion of the Overlap Group, see Scott E. Masten, "Old School Ties: Financial Aid Coordination and the Governance of Higher Education," *Journal of Economic Behavior & Organization* 28, no. 1 (1995): 23–48.

5. See Teresa Tritch, "Borrowing to Bridge the Gap: Where to Turn When Financial Aid or Savings Don't Cover Your College Costs," *Money*, September 10, 1990, 52. There were a few exceptions, the most important of which was the New York State Regents Scholarship program, where grants went to students who passed a certain threshold in standardized tests, but the amount students received still depended on their financial need. Those who were relatively wealthy received only an honorific amount, and the program was limited to those New York State residents who also attended a college in New York State. The National Merit Scholarship program remains the only national-level merit-aid program. There were roughly 10,000 awards in 2012 against approximately 20 million students in colleges and universities. The standard award in 2012 was $2,500. See National Merit Scholarship Corporation, "National Merit Scholarship Program," last updated September 2014, http://www.nationalmerit.org/nmsp.php#winner.

6. See College Board, *Trends in Student Aid, 2013* (College Board, 2014). The big increase in aid has been for graduate students, doubling in real terms over the same period to $53,000 per student in 2012–2013. That aid goes disproportionately to science and health care students.

7. For the details on athletic scholarships, see Statistic Brain, "NCAA College Athletics Statistics," April 26, 2014, http://www.statisticbrain.com/ncaa-college-athletics-statistics/.

8. National Labor Relations Board, "NLRB Director for Region 13 Issues Decision in Northwestern University Athletes Case," March 26, 2014, http://www.nlrb.gov/news-outreach/news-story/nlrb-director-region-13-issues-decision-northwestern-university-athletes.

9. James L. Shulman and William G. Bowen, *The Game of Life: College Sports and Educational Values* (Princeton, NJ: Princeton University Press, 2002).

10. Peter Cappelli and Shinjae Won, "How You Pay Affects How You Do: Financial Aid and College Outcomes" (Wharton School Management Department discussion paper, 2015).

11. Regula Geel and Uschi Backes-Gellner, "Earning While Learning: When and How Student Employment Is Beneficial," *Review of Labour Economics and Industrial Relations* 26, no. 3 (2012): 313–340.

12. Board of Governors of the Federal Reserve System, *In the Shadow of the Great Recession: Experiences and Perspectives of Young Workers* (November 2014), 14.

13. The federal government provides information on interest rates on loans at http://www.direct.ed.gov/calc.html.

14. See Jesse Rothstein and Cecilia Elena Rouse, "Constrained After College: Student Loans and Early-Career Occupational Choices," *Journal of Public Economics* 95 (2011): 149–163.

15. See Federal Student Aid, "Forgiveness, Cancellation, and Discharge," https://studentaid.ed.gov/repay-loans/forgiveness-cancellation (accessed October 2014).

16. The chart was compiled by The Institute for College Access and Success, "Despite Lower Rates, More Than 650,000 Defaulted on Federal Student Loans" (press release, Washington, DC, September 24, 2014).

17. The current level of student debt is keeping down house buying for this generation. Neil Irwin, "How Student Debt May Be Stunting the Economy," *New York Times*, May 14, 2014.

18. Deb Weinstein, "No Job and $50,000 in Student Debt. Now What?," *Forbes*, February 23, 2010, http://www.forbes.com/2010/02/23/student-loan -debt-payment-deferral-personal-finance-career-change.html.

19. The federal government has a relatively new loan program called Plus loans, primarily for graduate students, but parents of undergrads can tap into it. The student and his or her family must be eligible for financial aid, and the parent must have a good credit history. The good news is that the amount one can borrow is much higher. The bad news is that these loans are more like private loans: They charge a loan origination fee, currently 4.3 percent of the loan, and the interest rate of 7.2 percent through 2015 is pretty high, more than double the home mortgage rate on fifteen-year mortgages.

20. See Consumer Financial Protection Bureau, "CFPB Report Finds Distressed Private Student Loan Borrowers Driven into Default," October 16, 2014, http://www.consumerfinance.gov/newsroom/cfpb-report-finds-distressed -private-student-loan-borrowers-driven-into-default/.

21. See *Trends in College Pricing* (Princeton, NJ: The College Board, 2014).

22. Catharine B. Hill and Gordon C. Winston, "Access: Net Prices, Afford-ability, and Equity at a Highly Selective College," *Economics of Education Review* 24 (2005): 85–95.

23. Ron Lieber, "Appealing to a College for More Financial Aid," *New York Times*, April 4, 2014.

24. Scott Jaschik, "Feeling the Heat: The 2013 Survey of College and University Admissions Directors," *Inside Higher Ed*, September 18, 2013, http://www.insidehighered.com/news/survey/feeling-heat-2013-survey-college -and-university-admissionsdirectors.

25. Larry D. Singell Jr., "Merit, Need, and Student Self Selection: Is There Discretion in the Packaging of Aid at a Large Public University?," *Economics of Education Review* 21 (2002): 445–454.

5. Getting That First Job After College

1. Peter Cappelli, *Why Good People Can't Get Jobs: The Skills Gap and What Companies Can Do About It* (Philadelphia: Wharton Business School Press, 2013).

2. See, for example, David Finegold and Geoff Mason, "National Training Systems and Industrial Performance: U.S.-European Matched Plant Comparisons," *Research in Labor Economics*, 18 (1999): 3321–3358.

3. For a review of prior studies and some contemporary evidence, see Vera Brenčič, "Do Employers Respond to the Costs of Continued Search?," *Oxford Bulletin of Economics & Statistics* 72, no. 2 (2010): 221–245.

4. It is certainly possible to have such specific job requirements that there is no market for them. But if that is the case, we would expect the employer to be growing them from within: Who else would have any interest in producing them?

5. For information on the distribution of employers by size, see U.S. Census Bureau, "Statistics About Business Size (Including Small Business) from the U.S. Census Bureau," https://www.census.gov/econ/smallbus.html (accessed October 2014).

6. References and additional information on the topic of skill issues can be found in Peter Cappelli, "Skill Shortages, Skill Gaps, and Skill Mismatches: Evidence and Argument for the US," *ILR Review*, April 2015.

7. National Commission on Excellence in Education, "A Nation at Risk: The Imperative for Educational Reform" (Washington, DC: U.S. Department of Education, 1983).

8. National Center on Education and the Economy, "America's Choice: High Skills or Low Wages! The Report of the Commission on the Skills of the American Workforce" (Rochester, NY: 2009).

9. See Mary Joyce and David Neumark, "School-to-Work Programs: Information from Two Surveys," *Monthly Labor Review* 124 (2001): 38–50; and Peter Cappelli, *Employer Participation in School-to-Work Activities and Involvement with Schools*, The National Center for Postsecondary Improvement (Palo Alto, CA: Stanford University, 2001).

10. Elizabeth G. Chambers Mark Foulon, Helen Handfield-Jones, Steven M. Hankin, and Edward G. Michaels, "The War for Talent," *McKinsey Quarterly* (1998): 44–57.

11. U.S. Chamber of Commerce, "The State of American Business 2006" (Washington DC, 2006).

12. President's Council on Jobs and Competitiveness, *Roadmap to Renewal* (Washington, DC: The White House, 2012), http://www.jobs-council.com /recommendations/summary-of-road-map-to-renewal-report/.

13. Anthony P. Carnevale, Nicole Smith, and Jeff Strohl, *Help Wanted: Projections of Jobs and Education Requirements Through 2018* (Washington, DC: Center on Education and the Workforce, Georgetown University, 2010).

14. Lauren Weber and Melissa Korn, "Where Did All the Entry-Level Jobs Go?," *Wall Street Journal*, August 6, 2014.

15. See Committee on Science, Engineering, and Public Policy, *Rising Above the Gathering Storm: Energizing and Employing America for a Brighter Economic Future* (Washington, DC: National Academies Press, 2007); and also President's Council of Advisors on Science and Technology, 2012, http://www.whitehouse .gov/sites/default/files/microsites/ostp/pcast-engage-to-excel-final_2-25-12.pdf for the shortage view; Robert Charette, "The STEM Crisis Is a Myth" (IEEE Spectrum, August 2013), http://spectrum.ieee.org/at-work/education/the-stem -crisis-is-a-myth; and Hal Salzman, Daniel Kuehn, and B. Lindsay Lowell, "Guest-workers in the High-Skill US Labor Market" (EPI Briefing Paper No. 359, Washington, DC, April 24, 2013) for the surplus view.

16. Evidence on the distribution of students across college majors is in Bachelor's degrees conferred by degree-granting institutions, by field of study. NCES, *Digest of Education Statistics*, 2012, table 313.

17. Data for the beginning of the twenty-first century is in John Tsapogas, "Employment Outcomes of Recent Science and Engineering Graduates Vary by Field of Degree and Sector of Employment" (National Science Foundation InfoBrief NSF 04-316, May 2004), http://www.nsf.gov/statistics/infbrief /nsf04316/. Evidence as to why engineers leave the field is in Lisa Frehill, "Satisfaction: Why Do People Give Up Engineering? Surveys of Men and Women Engineers Tell an Unexpected Story," *Today's Engineer* (IEEE-USA), February 2010, http://www.todaysengineer.org/2010/Feb/satisfaction.asp. My study of IT workers is Peter Cappelli, "Why Is It So Hard to Find Information Technology Workers?," *Organizational Dynamics* 30, no. 2 (2001): 87–99.

18. I review the evidence from employers on this topic in *Why Good People Can't Get Jobs*. An outline of the range of behaviors that employers complain about is in Peter Cappelli, "Rethinking the 'Skills Gap,'" *California Management Review* 37, no. 4 (1995): 108–124. For arguments that these behaviors are really skills that can be taught, see Tim Kautz, James J. Heckman, Ron Diris, Bas ter Weel, and Lex Borghans, "Fostering and Measuring Skills: Improving Cognitive

and Non-Cognitive Skills to Promote Lifetime Success" (NBER Working Paper No. 20749, 2014).

19. See "The Skills and Qualities Employers Value Most in Their New Hires" (press release, Bethlehem, PA, National Association of Colleges and Employers, 2014).

20. Ofer Malamud, "Breadth vs. Depth: The Timing of Specialization in Higher Education" (NBER Working Paper 15943, 2010).

21. Eric A. Hanushek, Ludger Woessmann, and Lei Zhang, "General Education, Vocational Education, and Labor-Market Outcomes over the Life-Cycle" (NBER Working Paper No. 17504, October 2011).

22. "Temporary, Unregulated and Often Unpaid, the Internship Has Become the Route to Professional Work," *Economist*, September 6, 2014, http://www .economist.com/news/international/21615612-temporary-unregulated-and -often-unpaid-internship-has-become-route.

23. The *New York Times* has written a number of stories documenting these unpaid internships. See, for example, "Do Unpaid Internships Exploit College Students?," *New York Times*, February 4, 2012, http://www.nytimes.com /roomfordebate/2012/02/04/do-unpaid-internships-exploit-college-students.

24. Blair Hickman and Jeremy B. Merrill, "Unpaid Interns Win Major Ruling in 'Black Swan' Case—Now What?," *ProPublica*, June 12, 2013, http://www.propublica .org/article/unpaid-interns-win-major-ruling-in-black-swan-case-now-what.

25. See National Association of College and Employers, "Employers Hiring More Bachelor's Degree-Level Students for Internships and Co-ops," April 16, 2014, https://www.naceweb.org/s04162014/intern-co-op-hiring.aspx?land -intern-lp-1-spot-inhir-05092014.

26. See Glassdoor Team, "Top 20 Highest Rated Companies Hiring Interns Right Now," *Glassdoor Blog*, February 15, 2013, http://www.glassdoor.com/blog /top-20-highest-rated-companies-hiring-interns/.

27. Philip D. Gardner, Georgia T. Chao, and Jessica T. Hurst, "Ready for Prime Time? How Internships and Coops Affect Decisions on Full-Time Job Offers" (white paper prepared for monstertrak.com, 2008).

28. See, e.g., Barry Bosworth, *Certificates Count: An Analysis of Sub-baccalaureate Certificates* (Washington, DC: Complete College America, 2010).

29. Peter Cappelli and J. R. Keller, "A Study of the Extent and Causes of Alternative Work Arrangements," *ILR Review* 66, no. 4 (2013): 874–900.

30. See Board of Governors of the Federal Reserve System, *In the Shadow of the Great Recession: Experiences and Perspectives of Young Workers* (November 2014).

Conclusions

1. For an encyclopedic account of these benefits, see Ernest T. Pascarella and Patrick T. Terenzini, *How College Affects Students* (New York: Wiley, 2005).

Index

Credit: Amanda Stevenson

Peter Cappelli is the George W. Taylor Professor of Management at The Wharton School and director of Wharton's Center for Human Resources. He is also a research associate at the National Bureau of Economic Research. Cappelli has long been involved in federal government policy-making regarding the workforce and education, as codirector of the U.S. Department of Education's National Center on the Educational Quality of the Workforce, and as a member of the Executive Committee of the U.S. Department of Education's National Center on Post-Secondary Improvement at Stanford University. He lives in Philadelphia, PA.

PublicAffairs is a publishing house founded in 1997. It is a tribute to the standards, values, and flair of three persons who have served as mentors to countless reporters, writers, editors, and book people of all kinds, including me.

I. F. STONE, proprietor of *I. F. Stone's Weekly*, combined a commitment to the First Amendment with entrepreneurial zeal and reporting skill and became one of the great independent journalists in American history. At the age of eighty, Izzy published *The Trial of Socrates*, which was a national bestseller. He wrote the book after he taught himself ancient Greek.

BENJAMIN C. BRADLEE was for nearly thirty years the charismatic editorial leader of *The Washington Post*. It was Ben who gave the *Post* the range and courage to pursue such historic issues as Watergate. He supported his reporters with a tenacity that made them fearless and it is no accident that so many became authors of influential, best-selling books.

ROBERT L. BERNSTEIN, the chief executive of Random House for more than a quarter century, guided one of the nation's premier publishing houses. Bob was personally responsible for many books of political dissent and argument that challenged tyranny around the globe. He is also the founder and longtime chair of Human Rights Watch, one of the most respected human rights organizations in the world.

.   .   .

For fifty years, the banner of Public Affairs Press was carried by its owner Morris B. Schnapper, who published Gandhi, Nasser, Toynbee, Truman, and about 1,500 other authors. In 1983, Schnapper was described by *The Washington Post* as "a redoubtable gadfly." His legacy will endure in the books to come.

Peter Osnos, *Founder and Editor-at-Large*